WHAT DISNEY FANS ARE SAYING ABOUT
JEFF BARNES AND BEYOND THE WISDOM OF WALT

"Jeff's first book impacted the lives of so many people with Disney pixie dust and a new perspective to familiar stories. This valuable sequel continues to add to that magic with even more insights but this time into the Magic Kingdom and those who made Walt's final dream a reality. Disney cast members once ended their interactions with guests with the phrase, 'May all your days be Disney days!' This book will guarantee that wish can come true for every reader."

— Jim Korkis, Disney Historian and author of The Vault of Walt series

"I've spent the majority of my Emmy-winning baseball broadcasting career covering Hall of Famers. Jeff Barnes is an author who is in a league of his own. *Beyond the Wisdom of Walt* is the best Disney book I have ever read. A grand slam!"

— Ed Lucas, Emmy Award-Winning Yankee Broadcaster
and author of *Seeing Home*

"Like my days playing Tom Sawyer at Disneyland, I didn't want *Beyond the Wisdom of Walt* to end. Walt Disney World and EPCOT was Walt's biggest dream. Learn how you can make your biggest dreams come true by reading Jeff's best book yet!"

— Tom Nabbe, Disneyland's Original Tom Sawyer, Disney Legend,
and author of *From Disneyland's Tom Sawyer to Disney Legend*

"Jeff Barnes has done it again. By using a physical space, in this case the history of Walt Disney World, Barnes has knit together an extraordinary story dealing with the intangibles of personal motivation and the possibilities for the future. After reading *Beyond the Wisdom of Walt*, I know there is nothing that can stop me from achieving my dreams."

— Sam Gennawey, author of *The Disneyland Story,*
Walt Disney and the Promise of Progress City,
Universal vs. Disney, and *JayBangs*

"When Jeff Barnes wrote *The Wisdom of Walt*, he added to the Disneyland canon a unique take on the park. He has done the same, and more, with *Beyond the Wisdom of Walt*. Do your dreams a favor and read this book!"

— Bill Butler and Garner Holt of Garner Holt Productions, the world's largest maker of Audio-Animatronics

"Dr. Disneyland has done it again! In *The Wisdom of Walt*, Jeff Barnes shared lessons in leadership inspired by Walt Disney and America's first theme park, Disneyland. In this new book, Jeff goes beyond the berm of Walt's original Magic Kingdom to share with us lessons in pursuing our dreams inspired by "The Place Where Dreams Come True"—Walt Disney World. With examples from every corner of Walt Disney World and topics ranging from managing your time and overcoming obstacles to communicating clearly and leaving a legacy, *Beyond the Wisdom of Walt* offers success lessons for all of us. Read this book and let Jeff Barnes help you make your dreams come true!"

— Lou Prosperi, author of *The Imagineering Pyramid*

"With each page, I felt like Walt was speaking to me. I was encouraged to believe in myself and take that chance. Don't spend the next thirty years in a comfortable career; chase those dreams and do something to change your life and the lives of others! *Beyond the Wisdom of Walt* lights that fire that is inside all of us!"

— Mike Rahlmann, Host of *Be Our Guest* WDW Podcast—Top 10 Places & Travel Podcast on Apple Podcasts, named Top Disney-focused travel agent by readers of *The Unofficial Guide to Walt Disney World*—2017

"Once again, Barnes masterfully blends life and leadership lessons with Disney lore. This is thirteen chapters of inspiration, practical advice, and Disney perspective. This is storytelling at its best."

— Dr. Christopher W. Tremblay, author of *Walt's Pilgrimage*

"*The Wisdom of Walt* vs. *Beyond the Wisdom of Walt*? It's like a choice between Disneyland and Walt Disney World...BOTH are AWESOME!"

— Dan Sisneros, author of *Disney Tale of the Tape: Theme Park Boxing*

BEYOND THE WISDOM OF WALT

LIFE LESSONS FROM
THE MOST MAGICAL PLACE ON EARTH

JEFFREY A. BARNES

AVIVA
PUBLISHING

Published by:
Kidder Bombay Books
an imprint of Aviva Publishing
Lake Placid, NY
518-523-1320
www.AvivaPubs.com

Jeff Barnes
Email: jeff@thewisdomofwalt.com
www.thewisdomofwalt.com

Beyond the Wisdom of Walt, The Wisdom of Walt, and Aviva Publishing
are not associated with The Walt Disney Company.

ISBN: 978-1-944335-83-0

Library of Congress Control Number: 2017911425

Editor: Tyler Tichelaar, Superior Book Productions
Cover Designers: Kyle Ready and Nicole Gabriel
Interior Book Layout: Choi Messer

Every attempt has been made to source properly all quotes.
Printed in the United States of America
First Edition

2 4 6 8 10 12

To Niki, the only dream that mattered.
And to my Mom and Dad, for giving me "The World" in August 1974.

"Everyone in the world will come to these gates. Why? Because they want to look at the world of the future. They want to see how to make better human beings. That's what the whole thing is about. The cynics are already here and they're terrifying one another. What Disney is doing is showing the world that there are alternative ways to do things that can make us all happy. If we can borrow some of the concepts of Disneyland and Disney World and Epcot, then indeed the world can be a better place."

— Ray Bradbury

"[I]t seems unlikely that any American school of architecture will ever again graduate a student without first requiring him to take a field trip to Orlando."

— Peter Blake, architecture critic

US DISNEY THEME PARK DEDICATIONS

Disneyland

"To all who come to this happy place: Welcome. Disneyland is your land. Here, age relives fond memories of the past, and here youth may savor the challenge and promise of the future. Disneyland is dedicated to the ideals, the dreams, and the hard facts that have created America, with the hope that it will be a source of joy and inspiration to all the world."

— Walt Disney, July 17, 1955

Walt Disney World/Magic Kingdom

"Walt Disney World is a tribute to the philosophy and life of Walter Elias Disney...and to the talents, the dedication, and the loyalty of the entire Disney organization that made Walt Disney's dream come true. May Walt Disney World bring Joy and Inspiration and New Knowledge to all who come to this happy place...a Magic Kingdom where the young at heart of all ages can laugh and play and learn—together."

— Roy O. Disney, October 25, 1971

Epcot Center

"To all who come to this place of joy, hope and friendship, welcome.

EPCOT Center is inspired by Walt Disney's creative genius. Here, human achievements are celebrated through imagination, the wonders of enterprise, and concepts of a future that promises new and exciting benefits for all.

May EPCOT Center entertain, inform and inspire. And, above all, may it instill a new sense of belief and pride in man's ability to shape a world that offers hope to people everywhere."

— E. Cardon Walker, October 24, 1982

Disney-MGM Studios

"The World you have entered was created by The Walt Disney Company and is dedicated to Hollywood—not a place on a map, but a state of mind that exists wherever people dream and wonder and imagine, a place where illusion and reality are fused by technological magic. We welcome you to a Hollywood that never was—and always will be."

— Michael D. Eisner, May 1, 1989

Disney's Animal Kingdom

"Welcome to a kingdom of animals...real, ancient and imagined: a kingdom ruled by lions, dinosaurs and dragons; a kingdom of balance, harmony and survival; a kingdom we enter to share in the wonder, gaze at the beauty, thrill at the drama, and learn."

— Michael D. Eisner, April 22, 1998

Disney's California Adventure

"To all who believe in the power of dreams...Welcome! Disney's California Adventure opens its golden gates to you. Here we pay tribute to the dreamers of the past...the native people, explorers, immigrants, aviators, entrepreneurs and entertainers who built the Golden State. And we salute a new generation of dreamers who are creating the wonders of tomorrow...from the silver screen to the computer screen...from the fertile farmlands to the far reaches of space. Disney's California Adventure celebrates the richness and the diversity of California...its land, its people, its spirit and above all, the dreams that it continues to inspire."

— Michael D. Eisner, February 8, 2001

CONTENTS

A NOTE TO THE READER

LIKE *THE WISDOM OF WALT*, *Beyond the Wisdom of Walt* is not an academic work but one for the general reader. Just as the Imagineers wouldn't have wanted to destroy the magic of riding Space Mountain by stopping the roller coaster and turning on the lights to explain their research into roller coasters, display their blueprints, and explain why space travel is depicted the way that it is in a Tomorrowland theme park attraction, I didn't want to interrupt the reading process with needless footnotes and references to other resources. However, all the information contained in this book may be relied upon as accurate and derived from the sources found in the bibliography at the end.

Also note that this is not a biography of Walt Disney or any of the other Disney team members who continued his legacy after his death in December 1966. Nor is it a history of Disneyland or Walt Disney World. Rather, it is an inspirational and motivational text that may well employ mythology to move the narrative forward. When there are varying accounts of the same story, the author chose to use the version that best illustrates the leadership lesson in play.

As Mark Twain once said, and Walt Disney often quoted (supposedly), "Never let the facts get in the way of a good story." Even with myths—maybe more so—sometimes the "truth" of the story is more important than the facts of the story.

Lastly, a note on nomenclature. In general, EPCOT refers to Walt Disney's original dream for an Experimental Prototype Community of Tomorrow. Epcot Center refers to what opened at Walt Disney World on October 1, 1982—known today simply as Epcot. For the ease of the reader, the author is using EPCOT when referring to Walt's original dream and Epcot when referring to the theme park (regardless of year). Quotes from other sources use the nomenclature from those sources.

Enjoy!

FOREWORD

DON'T READ THIS BOOK UNLESS you are interested in learning many important lessons about leadership, management, technology, guest and customer service, and the excitement and fear involved in taking risks that lead to a better world for others and guarantee you will leave a legacy like Walt did.

All of these things will be taught to you by the master himself, Walt Disney, through the wonderful storytelling of Jeff Barnes.

You will learn the importance of setting higher and higher expectations for yourself and for others. Too many people in the world underestimate what they can achieve and underestimate the positive impact they can have on others. Walt had a real talent for communicating with clarity what he wanted and how he wanted it. This is an area we can all improve in, in all parts of our lives.

Walt's success was created by his enormous, positive, can do attitude and his passion for what he was doing. These two things are more important than anything else you need to move from a good life to a great life or even from a great life to an even greater life. It is never too late to get better or get started.

I would say the other things that made Walt and the Disney Company so successful are pure out hard work and persistence.

One thing that struck me in *Beyond the Wisdom of Walt* was that Walt clearly knew that many things in life are hard, but he also knew he could not be stopped because everything in life is hard before it is easy. Excellence is a state of mind, and Walt clearly had it. It is easy to be good, but very hard to be great.

Another thing that is clear in this book is that Walt knew better than anyone not to get bored with the basics. As he often said, "Keep it clean and friendly and everything will work out fine." This is a great lesson for all of us in this age when we believe technology is the answer to everything.

Walt totally understood what he wanted when he created a place where fantasy is real and reality is fantastic. Walt clearly understood that everything matters so taking shortcuts is the beginning of the end.

I was responsible for Walt Disney World® Operations for ten years and thought I knew just about everything. Reading this book once again reminded me that there is always more to learn and that good enough is not good enough.

My final advice is for you not only to read *Beyond the Wisdom of Walt*, but to study it and think about how you can implement Walt's lessons into your own life. And remember, as Walt said, "All of our dreams can come true if we have the courage to pursue them."

Take risks or take the agony of regrets! Take the time to plan the life you want, or spend a lot of time living the life you do not want. Have fun learning how Walt left a legacy and how you can too.

—Lee Cockerell
Executive Vice President (Retired and Inspired), Walt Disney World® Resort and author of *Creating Magic, The Customer Rules, Time Management Magic,* and *Career Magic*

INTRODUCTION
WELCOME TO THE WORLD WHERE DREAMS COME TRUE

WHEN YOU DRIVE ONTO THE vast Disney property in central Florida, the first sign that greets you proclaims, "Walt Disney World—The Place Where Dreams Come True." Every time I see this sign, I think back to my first trip to a Disney park. It was at Walt Disney World, in August 1974, that I rode my first monorail, first stepped onto Main Street, U.S.A., and first fell in love.

No, not *that* kind of love. I was only ten years old.

I fell in love with the magic.

I fell in love with the imagination. The hope. The spark of possibility that comes when you dream of a bigger and better world.

Since that first visit, I have lived in the best of both worlds. I grew up in Florida and enjoyed many trips to Walt Disney World's Magic Kingdom. As an adult, I have spent most of my years in California, and I currently live in Southern California where my wife, Niki, and I go to Disneyland, Walt's original Magic Kingdom, on a weekly basis.

Some people say we are "living the dream." And we are!

But what if? What if Walt Disney World isn't just a place where "dreams come true"? What if there could be more to life than looking forward to another day at Disneyland? More than forty years after first stepping foot inside a Disney park, I have bigger dreams than spending another day at Disney. Yet I keep going back.

Again. And again. And again....

XX   BEYOND THE WISDOM OF WALT

Why? Because I believe the experience inside the parks is the ultimate source of motivation and inspiration for making our *own* dreams come true. I believe the parks are showing us how to make those dreams a reality. To paraphrase a line from history, some see the world and ask, "Why?" I see Walt Disney World and ask, "Why not?"

And that's why we're here.

Deep down inside, you, too, have a dream. I wrote my first book, *The Wisdom of Walt*, because I believe it is possible to live every day like a day at Disneyland—days where you are doing what you have always dreamed, living your own great story, and making your own magic for the people you love. Just like Walt's first park wasn't big enough to hold all his dreams, *The Wisdom of Walt* wasn't big enough to cover everything we need to know about making our own dreams come true.

The purpose of *Beyond the Wisdom of Walt* is to do just that—go beyond the original book—and also to go beyond Walt Disney and Disneyland. Even though Walt did not live to see groundbreaking in Florida (1967), let alone the first park's opening (Magic Kingdom in 1971), his dream and vision had a tremendous influence on the final Florida project, and his spirit still influences decisions made there today. Likewise, we will find Walt present in *Beyond the Wisdom of Walt*—just not quite as much. Our focus is on the leaders and Imagineers inside Disney who have kept Walt's dream alive and helped keep the company moving forward during these last five decades.

Just as Walt Disney World's first park, the Magic Kingdom, follows the same basic layout as Disneyland, *Beyond the Wisdom of Walt* will follow the same format as its predecessor. Each chapter has a lead quote and starts with a story from one of the parks. Not every quote, however, comes from Walt Disney. Some stories still come from Disneyland, but most are from Walt Disney World. We are, after all, aiming to go *beyond* the wisdom of Walt!

Each chapter also includes what readers loved most about the original—a Souvenir Stop where you can apply the lessons you've learned in these pages to your own life, dreams, and success—and a Handstamp Story. Handstamp Stories are designed to have a bit of "magic," thus leaving you with an emotional memory of that chapter's lesson.

Though I live in Southern California and frequent Disneyland more often, my love and appreciation for the parks on both coasts has grown because of writing this book. You will soon discover that the stories behind Walt Disney World are as interesting as those of Disneyland, maybe even more so.

Like Walt Disney, I believe in the power of dreams. I especially believe in the power of your dreams. Just like Walt Disney, you *can* change your world. You can change your world using wisdom and inspiration from Walt's final dream, Walt Disney World. This book is your key to the world—the world where you see your own dreams come true. What are we waiting for?

Let the Magic Begin!

EXPANDING YOUR EXPECTATIONS

"There are thousands of mountains in the world...
there is only one Fujiyama.
There are innumerable architectural gems in the world...
there is only one Taj Mahal.
There are thousands of athletic events...
there is only one Olympics.
There are countless parks and entertainment sites
throughout the world...
there is only one Disneyland."

— Van Arsdale France
Creator of Disney University and Disney Legend

JUST GETTING STARTED

On July 17, 1965, a standing room only crowd gathered inside the Magnolia Room at the Disneyland Hotel. They were celebrating a happy event for "The Happiest Place on Earth." Disneyland, Walt Disney's dream that many believed would never survive six months, was celebrating ten years of unparalleled success.

Taking the stage together, Walt and Roy Disney talked briefly about the obstacles they had overcome a decade earlier and thanked everyone for making the impossible, possible. Walt shifted quickly from the past and focused on the future, "[W]e're just getting started. So, if any of you start to rest on your laurels, I mean, just forget it."

On that evening, Walt Disney's "Great Big Beautiful Tomorrow" was never grander. He used the rest of that happy evening to talk up plans for forty million dollars' worth of expansion at Disneyland over the next five years. Great Moments with Mr. Lincoln, fresh from the New York World's Fair, was already playing on Main Street, U.S.A., and soon enough, "it's a small world" would be found in Fantasyland.

New Orleans Square, Disneyland's first new themed land since the park opened in 1955, was already under construction. The Haunted Mansion had been standing, expectantly, since 1963, waiting for its happy haunts. Pirates of the Caribbean, delayed so Imagineers could switch it from a pedestrian, walk-through wax museum into a brilliant boat ride, would soon open and, according to former vice chairman of Walt Disney Imagineering, Marty Sklar, "ultimately become the most valuable single property ever created in the theme park business."

Walt ended the evening emphasizing the importance of tomorrow by highlighting a second complete redo of Disneyland's Tomorrowland. Scheduled for 1967, Walt's "World on the Move," would feature the WEDway PeopleMover and his all-time favorite attraction, another show from the New York World's Fair, the Carousel of Progress.

They really were *just* getting started.

And Walt Disney wasn't even talking about Disneyland. Yes, forty million dollars' worth of expansion in five years is impressive. Impressive enough to distract everyone from what Walt Disney was *really* doing in 1965.

Fewer than a dozen people in the room that night knew the truth—a truth that sat silent inside a hidden room thirty-three miles to the north, at the Disney Studio, in Burbank. Three people had a key. Seven more had seen its contents. Walt Disney was going to do what he *always* said he would never do.

A sequel.

Walt Disney was going to build *another* Disneyland.

A WHOLE NEW WORLD

WALT DISNEY CHANGED OUR WORLD. He changed our world by creating entirely new and different worlds. What was the key to Walt Disney's success? To Disneyland's success? It is the same key you and I hold today.

Imagination.

Disney's Magic Kingdoms remind us of magic. The magic of possibilities. Walt Disney was fond of saying, "It's kind of fun to do the impossible." Initially, Walt's dream for an amusement park was just that—impossible. Few remember it today, but Walt wanted to build his first amusement park, Mickey Mouse Park, on eight acres next to his studio in Burbank. When the city council turned him down, fearing a "carnival atmosphere" in their town, Walt was undeterred. He dreamed bigger and set his sights on an orange grove in Anaheim. Instead of eight acres, Walt now had 160 acres. Instead of a Mickey Mouse Park, Walt now dreamed of a place called Disneyland. After only a few years, 160 acres wasn't enough either. If 160 acres wasn't enough, imagine how limited and landlocked Walt would have felt if Burbank had said yes.

Too many of us live inside our heads. Our limited thinking limits our potential. All the world is a possibility, but our "Mickey Mouse lives" never expand beyond our original eight acres. Jonathan Fields tells us that, "[W]ords matter. Even the ones nobody hears but us. The ones uttered only in the cavernous reaches of our psyche. Especially those." Examples include:

I don't know how to start....

I can't do A because of B....

My dream isn't worth it....

I'm too scared to fail....

I'm too young....

I'm too old....

I always....

I never....

The thoughts you think and the words you use are shaping your story. If you want to change your world—*truly change your world*—then you first must change your thinking. Think big. Never stop dreaming, and expand your expectations. Walt Disney went from eight acres, to 160 acres, to 27,440 acres. How *big* can you go?

In his book, *Think Big, Act Bigger: The Rewards of Being Relentless*, Jeffrey Hayzlett talks about the importance of mindset and how we limit ourselves before we ever get started:

> I wanted to build my brand first online, so I told my team, "Go find out what I need to do to boost my social media presence by 25,000 fans on Facebook and Twitter as quickly as possible. Give me a plan for what I need to do, from increasing visibility to buying ads."
>
> They came back to me and said they could get only 15,000 fans on each.
>
> "Why?" I asked.
>
> "Our budget."
>
> "But I never *gave* you a budget! I just asked you to tell me *what it would take to get where we needed to go.*"
>
> Silence.
>
> [End scene. Cue crickets.]

How many times in your life does the scene end too soon and the only sound of success you hear is the sound of crickets chirping in the background—simply because you have placed unreal and imaginary limits on your life, your thinking, your success, and your dreams?

Throughout this book, I am going to challenge you to think a little *less* like Disneyland (charming) and a *lot more* like Walt Disney World (spectacular)!

> *"The first limitation that you have is your imagination. After that, the limitations are what is physically possible to build. It's surprising sometimes the things that you think are impossible that turn out to be doable and what you thought made them impossible was really an opinion. Not a fact."*

— Joe Rohde

THERE WILL NEVER BE ANOTHER DISNEYLAND

WALT DISNEY WORLD, THE WORLD's largest and most popular vacation destination, never would have been possible if Walt Disney had not let go of the limiting belief: "There will never be another Disneyland." After opening his dream to rave reviews in 1955, Walt soon found himself besieged by other cities that wanted their own slice of success. Over the next few years, Walt received hundreds of proposals for building another Disneyland, including invitations from Egypt, Japan, and Brazil. Never one to repeat himself, and abhorring sequels, Walt had zero interest in a Disneyland 2.0. He dismissed them out of hand, saying, "There will never be another Disneyland."

Eventually, success won out.

First, Disneyland's success transformed both Anaheim and Orange County, California. Overnight, the sleepy little farming town, founded by fifty German families in 1857, woke up one hundred years later to discover it was the most desirable tourist destination on the planet.

Everyone wanted to come to Disneyland.

While Walt enjoyed controlling everything inside the "berm" of his Magic Kingdom, he was equally horrified at the sudden squalor and "sea of sleaze" that surrounded him on Harbor Boulevard. Walt reminded everyone of this reality at Disneyland's Tencennial Celebration:

> [W]hen we opened, if we could have bought more land, we'd have bought it. Then we'd have had control and it wouldn't look too much like a second-rate Las Vegas around here. We could have had a better chance to control it. But we ran out of money. And then by the time that we did have a little money, everybody got wise to what was going on and we couldn't buy anything around the place at all.

Secondly, Walt loved seeing how much happiness his dream brought to people. Yet, even though everyone wanted to come to Disneyland, not everyone could. The world was less mobile in 1955. America's interstate highway system was two years away from construction and air travel was expensive. Seventy-five percent of the US population still lived east of the Mississippi River, but it accounted for only 8 percent of Disneyland's dramatic and unprecedented attendance.

Why should California have all the fun?

A question asked repeatedly when guests by the millions experienced Disney attractions for the first time on the East Coast at the 1964-65 New York World's Fair.

The solution to Walt's success was to do what he always warned against—a sequel. Nonetheless, Walt Disney was determined *not* to repeat himself. Roy Disney, Walt's older brother, recognized the creative quirkiness of his younger brother when he recounted, "Walt did not want to travel the same route twice. He was a peculiar guy that way. He always told me, 'If you do something well, how are you going to top yourself?'"

Walt did Disneyland well. Very well.

Knowing that he could never top himself, Walt's real focus in Florida, first called "Project X," then "Project Winter," then "The Florida Project," then "Disney World," and finally, "Walt Disney World," was EPCOT—Walt Disney's Experimental Prototype Community of Tomorrow. Walt not only hated repeating himself; he also hated standing still. His boredom with cartoon shorts brought him to full-length animated feature films. His boredom with animated feature films brought him to live-action movies. His boredom with live-action movies brought him to Disneyland—a place where guests stepped through the silver screen and into a series of stories—a place where guests were active participants rather than passive consumers—a place that Walt Disney, always a starter but rarely a finisher, was already bored with by 1960.

Now, what interested Walt most was the plight of America's inner cities. The master planner of Disneyland was ready to tackle what he knew would be his final frontier—urban planning. To realize his final dream—a "Progress City," a "City of Tomorrow," which he eventually called "EPCOT"—Walt expanded his own expectations and consented to building another Disneyland—Walt Disney World's Magic Kingdom. The theme park, necessary for funding what would be Walt's final wish, was only a small part of the original plan. Reflecting on Walt Disney World in 2016, *Life* magazine wrote:

> But Walt's real interest lay in the even more ambitious EPCOT, a fully functional, utopian city that would, he believed, change the way that people lived, thereby shaping civilization itself. In a nation rife with civil unrest, the ever-optimistic Walt felt that EPCOT could offer a corrective, becoming in the process his greatest achievement. "Fancy being remembered around the world for the invention of a mouse!" he exclaimed.

Regarding sequels, I can appreciate Walt's thinking. After realizing my dream of writing *The Wisdom of Walt*, I too was ready to move on to new and different projects. *All I need to do is sell a few copies and then I can declare, "Mission Accomplished!" and move on with the rest of my life!*

Or so I thought.

When developing my college course on The History of Disneyland, I claimed that Disneyland, *The Original*, is *the* Disney park with all the history, stories, inspiration, and motivation.

Nothing could be further from the truth.

Receiving a signed copy of David Koenig's book about Walt Disney World, *Realityland*, woke me up to the reality that yes, Disneyland is the original and will always be the only Disney park that Walt ever actually walked in. However, I now know that the reasons why Walt wanted to go to Florida, the process of acquiring the land, the crisis in leadership experienced by the organization following Walt's sudden passing in 1966—six months prior to groundbreaking in Florida, what it took to convert nearly unsaleable swampland into the Vacation Kingdom of the World and the Most Magical Place on Earth, what ultimately became of Walt's EPCOT, and hundreds of other stories are also fodder for lessons on life, leadership, and success—and they are equal to, if not greater than, what I explored in *The Wisdom of Walt*.

> *"He [Walt] used to get so God damn excited about EPCOT. When he talked about it, it was like he'd just come back from the moon yesterday. He was just so thrilled."*
>
> — Rolly Crump

A BLANK SHEET OF PAPER

IN HIS BOOK *DREAM IT! DO IT!*, Marty Sklar writes about the choice we have when looking at a blank sheet of paper, "You can see it as the most frightening thing in the world—because *you have to make the first mark* on it. Or you can see a blank page as the greatest opportunity—*you get to make the first mark* on it."

Walt Disney wanted 160 acres in Anaheim because he needed a blank page, a flat canvas where he could forge his own rivers, make his own mountains, and create his own castle. Now he was expanding his expectations and pushing for 27,440 acres of blank page and flat canvas in central Florida. One more time he wanted to forge his own rivers, make his own mountains, create his own castle...and *so much more*!

In *Walt Disney and the Promise of Progress City*, Sam Gennawey describes in detail the impressive scale model that Disney built to display Walt's vision for his Experimental Prototype Community of Tomorrow. Starting in 1967, guests who experienced General Electric's Carousel of Progress at Disneyland viewed this model following the show. Today, a portion of the model can still be seen when you ride the WEDway PeopleMover in Tomorrowland at Walt Disney World's Magic Kingdom:

Based on many of the drawings used during the EPCOT planning process, this huge model covers 6,900 square feet and measures 115 feet by 60 feet. Everything is built to the scale of one-eighth inch to the foot, and is incredibly detailed, with more than 4,500 structures, 22,000 scale shrubs and trees, and 1,400 working streetlights. Many of the buildings are lit from within. Some of the building interiors are even furnished. At the center of the model is a huge megastructure with a dome-like shape punctuated by skylights and a gleaming 30-story hotel tower.

The central city is surrounded by a greenbelt filled with a wide variety of structures: beautiful and sleek Mid-Century Modern civic buildings, an amusement park with spinning rides, and a lake with a Tiki restaurant on one edge. Surrounding this greenbelt are single-family homes and more parks. Way off in the distance is an atomic power plant. Look closely and you can see moving sidewalks and electric carts. Jet airplanes are seen leaving the Progress City airport.

> The model is fully animated. The transportation network—monorails, automobiles, and WEDway PeopleMovers—has 2,450 vehicles in constant motion. According to one 1967 press release, this model is not fantasy; it could "be built today through applications of the most advanced technologies." Plus, you get to experience an entire day in a matter of minutes at Progress City. The lighting begins during the day, but slowly turns into night. At one magic moment, all of the lights in the model come alive and the city becomes "a sparkling jewel."

Right now, think about your life, your dreams, and your success as a blank sheet of paper. Are you excited? Frightened? Both?

We were all born into this world as blank pieces of paper. We didn't have any beliefs…about anything. Over time, we started making marks on the page. Often, we turn our marker over to others and allow them to mark our pages. These marks become our beliefs, beliefs that start driving this bus called "life." We stop paying attention and rarely question where we are going or how we are getting there. Life goes on autopilot.

Let me give you three stories as examples. First, Dole Whip is one of the most popular and unique Disney treats on either coast. At Disneyland, Niki and I often see guests in Adventureland standing in a thirty-minute line, or longer, waiting to order their cups of pineapple perfection. Meanwhile, just a few feet away in the outdoor waiting area for the Tiki Room, you can order a Dole Whip from the *exact* same stand in three minutes or less. Every summer, we get to enjoy seeing students experience their first Dole Whips—they are always grinning from ear to ear while also shaking their heads in disbelief that they never noticed the second line, aka "the backside of Dole Whip."

Here's another example. In his book, *Stories from a Theme Park Insider*, Robert Niles tells the following story about guests waiting in line at the Magic Kingdom at Walt Disney World:

> Three cast members were "playing in the park" on their day off. For fun, they decided to queue up in front of the door to the riverboat crew's office, around the corner from the Hall of Presidents entrance, in Liberty Square. Sure enough, within a minute, a couple walked up to them.
>
> "What are you in line for?" the man asked.
>
> "I don't know, but we're first!" the leader of the three replied, while the others did their best to keep straight faces.
>
> The man turned to his partner, shrugged, and joined the "line."
>
> Within minutes on this busy summer day, two dozen others had joined the queue, which was now snaking toward the stockade that stands in front of the riverboat dock, about 20 yards away. When the line reached the riverboat's entrance, cutting off the path toward the Haunted Mansion, the original three grinned at one another and the leader nodded. He turned to the first man who'd joined the queue.
>
> "Darn it, it's almost time for our lunch reservations at the Diamond Horseshoe. Gotta go."
>
> With that, the three walked over to the Horseshoe, suppressing laughs the whole way. As they passed the riverboat dock, the leader waved at the riverboat greet,

whom he knew, and said, "I don't know what's going on, but the crowd here looks like it's actually a line waiting for something in front of the crew office over there. You better check it out."

The three ran for it, as the greeter walked over to the front crowd, wondering why a line would have formed in front of an unmarked (though well-themed) utility door.

"Excuse me, sir," he asked the man who'd first joined the queue, "but what do you think you are in line for?"

"I don't know," he replied.

"But I'm first!"

Lastly, when Niki and I went to Disneyland Paris in 2010, my favorite feature was the Discovery Arcade on Main Street. Instead of accepting the bottleneck that occurs at the American Parks, Imagineers created a stunning, themed alternate route behind the Main Street stores and restaurants. I spent hours exploring the Discovery Arcade, a space dedicated to the "golden age of invention with scale models of some of the 19th Century's greatest, ground breaking creations." Before our visit, I was unaware of the arcade so it was a real "Eureka!" I was so mesmerized that when we returned home to Hawaii, I used the Discovery Arcade as the model for theming our new university campus in Mililani.

Here's the kicker. It didn't dawn on me until *months* after we were home that there must be another arcade, running behind the shops and restaurants on the *other* side of Main Street. Sure enough, there is. It's called Liberty Arcade, and the only thing I know about it comes from the Disneyland Paris website:

Liberty Arcade: A Walk to Liberty

Discover the story of the Statue of Liberty, as you stroll along this beautiful, Liberty Arcade at Disneyland Paris lit by gas lanterns and built from ornate ironwork. Historic photographs, artwork and display cases illustrate the inception and construction of Lady Liberty in a tale that links France to the United States of America—you can even take part in the statue's inauguration at Statue of Liberty Tableau.

Because of my limited perspective, I missed the entire experience. A great reminder to liberate yourself from your limiting beliefs and discover your full potential.

> *"To a child, this weary world is brand-new, gift wrapped. Disney tried to keep it that way for adults."*

> — Eric Sevareid

WHERE DO WE BEGIN?

WALT WELCOMED THE BLANK PAGE. Once he let go of the idea that there would never be another Disneyland, he was ready to start over. Again. With his East Coast Disneyland, with EPCOT, he knew he needed to think new—differently:

I don't believe there's a challenge anywhere in the world that's more important to people everywhere than finding solutions to the problems of our cities.... But where do we begin? How do we start answering this great challenge? Well, we're convinced we must start with the public need, and the need is not just for curing the old ills of the old cities—we think the need is for starting from scratch on virgin land and building a special kind of new community.

Starting in the early 1960s, Walt considered projects and proposals in St. Louis, Niagara Falls, New York City, Baltimore, Washington, DC, and Palm Beach. Finding the exact East Coast location was a monumental task. He knew he needed access to a population center, an agreeable climate, and enough land to avoid the blight around Disneyland in Anaheim. What Walt found in central Florida was property that was "ordinary enough to be a blank page and simultaneously exotic enough to be picturesque and interesting." David Koenig tells us more in *Realityland*:

By November [1963], Walt realized it was time to make a move. He gathered onto the private plane Tatum, Walker, Price and the few other insiders he had let in on his plans. The pilot charted a course for St. Louis, where the city leaders still held out hope that Disney would change its mind. No, St. Louis wouldn't work. Too little land, too much financial risk. The plane continued on to Niagara Falls. Already the group could see that the winter would be too cold and last too long. The plane flew to a site between Washington, D.C., and Baltimore. The weather there, too, could be harsh.

Their only option was to head south. Walt asked the pilot to fly along the coast to make sure that he didn't want to build near the beach. The pilot finally headed inland, toward central Florida. Walt asked him to fly as low as possible, so he could get a good look at the expansive swamps and woodlands near Orlando. Before heading back to California, the plane stopped in town to refuel.

There, the group heard the news—President Kennedy had been shot.

During the flight home, every passenger sat in stunned silence. The nation's young, optimistic leader had been mortally shot in the middle of a Dallas city street. Was this the hopeful, productive America that Walt and his Disneyland celebrated and held up to the world as a shining example? Never before had the entire world so badly needed the promise of Walt's City of Tomorrow. He had no more time to waste. He'd made up his mind. Just before the plane touched down in Burbank, Walt broke the silence. "Well," he said, "that's the place—central Florida."

Once Walt had made his decision, acquiring the land necessary for building his Experimental Prototype Community of Tomorrow required a cloak-and-dagger operation that included disguises, dummy corporations, and the discretion of a former OSS Officer from World War II.

Why such secrecy?

Walt knew that if word got out that he was interested in doing anything in central Florida, especially on the size, scale, and scope of what the company ultimately proposed, then the worthless swampland would skyrocket in value. Walt and his team started with the expectation that they needed a minimum of 10,000 acres, but ultimately, they acquired more than 27,000 acres—twice the size of the island of Manhattan. At one point, Roy believed they had purchased enough parcels, so he balked at writing more checks for more acres. Walt countered, reminding Roy of how much opportunity they had lost by limiting themselves to a mere 160 acres in Anaheim in 1953. Roy relented and kept writing the checks.

Most of the property came from the purchase of three large parcels. However, to link the land together, hundreds of other owners, many of whom had never seen their land or even knew they owned it, had to be convinced to sell.

Isn't success funny? Walt Disney started out like most of us—a nobody from nowhere. At one point, he was homeless in Kansas City and eating beans out of a garbage can. The idea of owning land, any land, was a faraway dream. Back then, Walt simply wanted to know where his next meal was coming from and where he might be sleeping that evening.

Fast forward to 1963 and the Disney name is one of the most famous names in the world. Walt is so famous that he almost can't afford to purchase the worthless acres of swampland he needs in central Florida. His name is so synonymous with success that prices will skyrocket as land speculators endeavor to cash in on Walt's creative genius and ride his coattails. Coattails Walt never expected to have back when he couldn't even afford a coat!

> *"I didn't think this [Walt Disney World] was possible.*
> *When I went with him to buy the property here,*
> *it was a horrible piece of property, dust and everything,*
> *and he was excited about it. This was a big thing to do.*
> *God love him."*

> — Bill "Sully" Sullivan

SOUVENIR STOP

TRAIN YOUR BRAIN—NIKI AND I have been to Disneyland more than 500 times. You would think we have seen, and done, it all. We haven't. On each visit, we challenge each other to discover something we haven't yet seen or done. This keeps us sharp, interested, and engaged.

You can do the same. Over the next seven days, train your brain to "expand your expectations" by challenging yourself to see something you have never noticed. Try this on your drive to work, your way home from school, anywhere and everywhere you go.

> *"If you do what you've always done,*
> *you'll get what you've always gotten."*
>
> — Tony Robbins

BLANK BELIEFS—CHARLES SCHULTZ ONCE SAID, "Life is like a ten-speed bicycle. Most of us have gears we never use." In the exercise below, I want you to write down your ten most limiting beliefs and then turn them into empowering beliefs that reflect unlimited potential. To get you started, I am providing my own set of examples.

LIMITING BELIEFS	EMPOWERING BELIEFS
I don't know how to write a book.	I do know how to write a page, and a book is just a bunch of pages put together.
I hate exercising.	I love to eat *and* I like being healthy.
I am too old to speak to young people about their dreams and goals.	I have the experiences and stories young people need to hear about achieving their dreams and goals.
I will never be able to afford a Disney cruise.	I can set big revenue goals and align my expenses to reflect how much I value going on a Disney cruise.
I don't like cats.	I love Niki, who loves cats, so I can love cats too.
I don't have enough time to be an administrator, author, teacher, and speaker.	I can get up earlier, stay up later, and manage my schedule so that it reflects my dreams, goals, and values.

My desk is always messy.	I have organized other areas of my life, so I can do the same with my desk.
I have no patience.	I can take deep breaths and am in complete control of my responses and reactions.
I will never see one of my books for sale in a Disney park.	I will keep writing, promoting, and selling until Disney takes notice and begins selling *The Wisdom of Walt* series in all of its parks.
"I will never do anything as good as *Snow White*."	Oh wait, that isn't one of my limiting beliefs—Walt Disney once said that. At some level, we all struggle with limiting beliefs!

Use the ten blank spaces below to write down your ten most limiting beliefs.

1. _____
2. _____
3. _____
4. _____
5. _____
6. _____
7. _____
8. _____
9. _____
10. _____

Now, use the following ten spaces to reimagine your beliefs into positive statements that reflect the real you, real possibilities, and real unlimited potential.

1. _____
2. _____
3. _____
4. _____
5. _____
6. _____
7. _____
8. _____
9. _____
10. _____

*"Q: How many Imagineers does it take
to change a light bulb?
A: Who said it has to be a light bulb?"*

— Walt Disney Imagineering

BLOW UP YOUR GOAL—WALT WENT from eight acres, to 160 acres, to 27,440 acres. What space do you and your dream currently occupy? Set your goal for where you want to be one year from today:

_____
_____
_____
_____
_____

Now, take that goal and blow it up to ten times its size. This is now your *real* goal. Oh, and you have six months, not a full year.

Why? Because eight acres never inspired anyone to do anything. Being "realistic" never changed the world. When you expand your expectations—say, to 27,440 acres—then you are scared *and* excited. Mediocre is for the masses. Own your world by dreaming bigger than the world!

"If you set your goals ridiculously high and it's a failure,
you will fail above everyone else's success."

— James Cameron

GETTING YOUR HAND STAMPED

WHEN WALT DISNEY SELECTED ANAHEIM as the site for Disneyland, the good news was that it was in the middle of nowhere with lots of available and affordable land. The bad news was that it was in the middle of nowhere, with only 14,500 people and a scant sixty motel/hotel rooms. Knowing this wasn't enough, and that all his resources were tied up in constructing the park, Walt contacted national chains such as Sheraton, Hilton, and Marriott to see whether they wanted to invest in his dream and build an onsite hotel.

Everyone said no.

Soon, Disney was desperate. With excitement building for the park's grand opening, calls asking about overnight accommodations averaged as many as 800 per day. The one lone ranger willing to consider building a hotel was Walt's friend, Jack Wrather, producer of the TV shows *The Lone Ranger* and *Lassie*. Selling Wrather on the success of Disneyland and the prospective profits from an onsite hotel property wasn't easy, either. Stephanie Barczewski describes the scene in her book, *Magic Kingdoms: A History of the Disney Theme Parks*:

> Walt then invited his friend Jack Wrather, a Texas oil millionaire turned television producer who had recently entered the hotel business, to come and see the Disneyland construction site in 1954. Wrather, too, was initially skeptical that the park would succeed, and he initially said no when Walt asked him to build a hotel. But Walt pleaded with him—according to some accounts with tears in his eyes—and Wrather relented.

The Disneyland Hotel opened on October 5, 1955 with 104 rooms. Like Disneyland, it was an overnight success and required immediate expansion. In 1962, Wrather constructed the first of the three Disneyland Hotel towers. With the first tower at eleven stories, Walt was concerned that it would be visible from inside the park and an intrusion on his magical illusion. To assuage Walt's concerns, Wrather raised a balloon at the proposed tower site while Walt stood on the Mark Twain dock in his nineteenth century Frontierland. Walt relented, but just to be safe, he had New Orleans Square constructed as a strategic "screen" from the ever-rising realities of the outside world.

One of the most notable additions was the Disneyland Hotel monorail station in 1961. It transformed the monorail from a novel theme park attraction to the true mass-transit system Walt always wanted—a system replicated at Walt Disney World where it includes stops at the Grand Floridian and Polynesian Hotels, and *inside* the Contemporary Resort.

With more than thirty different onsite hotels, Walt Disney World's three hotels on the Seven Seas Lagoon monorail loop represent less than 10 percent of the available onsite accommodations. And to think that back in 1955, nobody wanted to build a hotel to support Walt's first park. Today, if you want to spend every night in a different room at the various Walt Disney World hotels, it will take you *more than seventy years* before you run out of rooms.

How much room will you need for your dream? Who knows? This is only the first chapter.

We're just getting started.

> *"Here in Florida we have something special we never enjoyed at Disneyland…the blessing of size. There's enough land here to hold all the ideas and plans we can possibly imagine."*
>
> — Walt Disney

LEARNING TO LET IT GO

*"If you focus on what you have left behind,
you will never be able to see what lies ahead."*

— Gusteau from *Ratoutille*

A FRIEND IN DEEDS

Above the Crystal Arts shop on Main Street, U.S.A. in Walt Disney World is a curious window. This, like many of the Main Street windows at Disneyland and Walt Disney World, is a tribute window—Walt's way of giving credit to the men and women who helped make his dreams possible. This particular pane pays homage to an "M. T. Lott." Who was M. T. Lott?

Nobody.

What did M. T. Lott ever do for Disney?

Nothing.

M. T. Lott never existed. Further, the window credits M. T. Lott with being in the real estate investment business even though M. T. Lott was never *real*. This is a fictitious business name, a clever Imagineering word play for "empty lot," which is exactly what the land where Walt Disney World sits today was back in the 1960s.

What the window really represents is the half-dozen dummy corporations Disney created to purchase the property, in secret, before announcing to the world that Disney was coming to central Florida. Subsidiaries of M. T. Lott include: Tomahawk Properties, Latin American Development, Ayefour (I-4) Corporation, Bay Lake Properties, Reedy Creek Ranch Lands, and Compass East Corporation. Donn Tatum, a Disney executive who served as Disney's chief executive officer following Roy Disney's death in 1971, is the real honoree here. He played a major role in acquiring the 27,440 acres, and his tongue-in-cheek tribute reads, "A Friend in Deeds is a Friend Indeed."

In 1965, it was indeed no secret that someone was purchasing large tracts of swampland south of Orlando. Speculation regarding who, and for what, ran rampant in the local media for months. Possible enterprises included an East Coast Disneyland, but most believed it was associated with either the aerospace industry or automobile manufacturing. The Big Reveal came on Sunday, October 24, 1965, when residents in the sleepy city awoke to a banner headline. Splashed across the top of the Sunday edition of the *Orlando Sentinel* were these words: **"We Say: 'Mystery' Industry is Disney."** Details were scant, but subheadlines show the *Sentinel* knew instantly that central Florida would never be the same:

"City to Become Hub for Millions of Tourists, Billions of Dollars"
"Disneyland Produces Fantastic Prosperity"
"City [EPCOT] Housing 10,000 People Will Be Built"

Walt had warned the handful of people within Disney who knew what the company was up to in central Florida that they would lose their jobs if they let word get out that Disney was indeed the buyer. Guess who let the secret slip?

Walt.

During Disneyland's Tencennial Celebration, the company treated the press to tours of Disneyland and one-on-one interviews with Walt. Following her tour, Emily Bavar of the *Orlando Sentinel* asked Walt directly whether he was the one purchasing large tracts of land in Orlando.

Walt froze.

"He looked like I had thrown a bucket of water in his face," Bavar recalled.

Trying to recover, Walt responded, "Why would we want to locate way out in that area?" He then gave Bavar a billion reasons why he wanted nothing to do with Orlando or central Florida.

The world's best storyteller was also the world's worst liar. Bavar believed it *was* Disney because Walt had never actually answered her question *and* he knew way too much about Orlando for a man with no interest in building there.

Once the news broke on October 24, things moved quickly. An official announcement was made the following day, and then Walt, Roy, and the Governor of Florida, Haydon Burns, held a press conference on November 15 at Orlando's Cherry Plaza Hotel. This was Walt's first public mention of his desire to build a "City of Tomorrow." Regarding the theme park, Walt reminded the Governor that he had always said, "There will never be another Disneyland," but that they had learned "an awful lot" over the past ten years and looked forward in Florida to "starting from scratch."

Thanks to Walt's gaff, prices on the remaining parcels jumped from an average of $183 an acre to $1,000. Disney only needed to acquire 300 acres more, however, so the total purchase price for all the land was about five million. Not bad for land eleven miles long, four miles wide, equal in size to San Francisco, and twice the size of the island of Manhattan.

I've never had a secret as large as the one Walt was keeping in 1965. At least not anything that involved 27,000 acres and $5 million. I have, however, done dumb things without the luxury of dummy corporations to help keep them hidden.

Have you ever wished that *you* could start over? Doesn't the idea of "starting from scratch" sound amazing?

But that's not life. When it comes to dreams and success, "M. T. Lott" is nowhere to be found. Our past isn't always pretty. Like Walt, our future doesn't always go as planned. Bad things happen. Sometimes, *really* bad things happen.

Then what?

The greatest danger in life isn't making a mistake, risking a relationship, or losing a loved one. All those things, and more, will happen regardless.

The greatest danger in life is staying stuck. Refusing to move forward. Frozen.

That's when you know it is time to let it go.

> *"Don't cling to a mistake just because you*
> *spent a long time making it."*
>
> — Aubrey De Graf

CATCH AND RELEASE

DISNEY TEACHES US TO DEAL with life's greatest challenges. Growing up, leaving childhood, finding purpose, adapting to change, and dealing with death are experiences every human being, regardless of culture, faces. Disney films face these realities, but the realities are evident in the parks as well.

Walt promised that Disneyland, "as long as there is imagination left in the world," would "never be finished." We love it when new attractions appear in the park. We hate it, however, when Disney removes the old to make way for the new. The Phantom Boats in Tomorrowland have the distinction of being the first attraction removed from a Disney park. They only lasted a little more than a year, August 1955-October 1956, so few guests remember them.

Many of my memories from Walt Disney World no longer exist. I will never again ride the Swan Boats with my grandmother (both are gone), ride free with my friends on If You Had Wings, or submerge with the submarines in Fantasyland. At Disneyland, my daughter and

I lament the loss of the Skyway, and people ask me, repeatedly, about the long-lost WEDway PeopleMover.

I get it.

But we forget that the parks aren't museums. When we focus on what was, we risk missing out on what *is*. I'm sure Nature's Wonderland was great, but was it better than Big Thunder Mountain—the attraction that replaced it? The same with Tomorrowland's Flying Saucers—a great memory, but were they better than a race through the cosmos on Space Mountain? Doubtful.

It's not just attractions, either. Shops, shows, parades, and activities come and go as well. For example, when Tom Sawyer Island opened in 1956, one of the activities was the opportunity to fish in Disneyland's Rivers of America. Tom Nabbe, employed by Walt at age fourteen to play the part of Tom Sawyer, tells us more in his book *From Disneyland's Tom Sawyer to Disney Legend*:

> Disney stocked the Rivers of America with plenty of catfish, bluegill, and sun perch, so guests had a pretty good chance of hooking a fish. When we first opened up Tom Sawyer Island, the policy was catch-and-clean. We had a little area to clean the fish if guests wanted to do that and had plastic bags to put the fish in. That only lasted a month or two because fish would start turning up in places where you didn't want old, dead, smelly fish—like trashcans throughout the park.

Can you imagine? Walking around Disneyland carrying a dead fish. As the day gets hotter, your dead fish gets smellier. But you hold on to it for dear life. A timeless souvenir from Tom Sawyer Island. How could you possibly consider letting such a priceless thing go?

You can't move forward with your future while simultaneously holding on to your dead past. Life is messy, especially when it involves human beings. Along the way, we make mistakes, have regrets, relationships break, and failures mount. These become our story, and we start believing that new narratives are no longer possible.

This isn't true.

Correction—it is true. But only if you continue to hold on to it.

Walking around with a dead fish at a Disney park is pointless. Yet that is exactly what we do with life. We carry on with the negative, destructive, painful things from our past, and not just for a few hours. This goes on for days, weeks, months, and years.

> *"It's sort of like not being able to enjoy sitting on your front porch anymore because it totally reeks of something foul out there. You can come up with all these brilliant ways to deal with the problem—light incense, set up fans, blame it on the dog—but until you realize that something has crawled under your house and died, your problems will linger on, stinking up your life."*

> — Jen Sincero

IT WAS LIKE THE END OF THE WORLD

WALT DISNEY NEVER WALKED IN the World that bears his name. The man who had the uncanny ability to look into the future and know what *we* needed was unable to see his own future. One year after the Orlando announcement, and six months before groundbreaking in Florida, Walt Disney died of lung cancer. He was a three-pack-a-day smoker. For those close to Walt, he was as famous for his smoking as he was for his success. In *Walt Disney: The Triumph of the American Imagination*, Neal Gabler goes into detail:

> He had smoked for years, since his days with the Red Cross in France, chain-smoking, nervously smoking, his fingers stained from the nicotine, his voice raw and hoarse, and

almost every conversation was punctuated frequently by his throat clearing. "I just can't picture him without a cigarette," Diane would recall.... Lillian said that Walt had "burned more furniture and more rugs and more everything with his cigarettes than anybody I ever knew," and Diane claimed that one could always identify Walt's butts in an ashtray because he would smoke the cigarettes down to the last quarter-inch, until he could barely hold them. "He would forget to put them out," she said. "He would light them and get carried away with what he was thinking about and just hold them. Sometimes he would hold them in his mouth or in his hand and get an ash on it two inches long."

He was often encouraged to quit.... Early in 1957, when Gunther Lessing celebrated his first anniversary of not having had a cigarette, Lessing made a point of telling Walt, but Walt wasn't interested. When doctors came to the studio to lecture the staff on the hazards of smoking, Walt wouldn't attend. One Christmas, Diane bought him two cartons of filtered cigarettes, thinking they would at least be better for him than the filterless ones he smoked, and Walt promised her he would use them. He just broke off the filters. "I didn't tell her *how* I would use them," he joked to a confederate. During one of his last meetings with him, Ward Kimball remembered Walt breaking into a long coughing jag. "When I timidly asked why he didn't give up smoking," Kimball said, "Walt looked up at me, his face still red from the coughing, and rasped, 'Well, I gotta have a few vices, don't I?'"

Walt Disney's vice caught up with him in November 1966. He was in terrible pain from an old polo injury and scheduled a long-delayed surgery at UCLA to repair the damage in his neck. However, during a pre-operative exam, doctors discovered something more disconcerting—a spot on Walt's left lung. They operated immediately and removed the malignant lung. Walt's prognosis wasn't good—he was given six months to two years to live. Instead, Walt Disney died in less than five weeks.

The world, including his family and his company, was in shock. The night before Walt's death, Roy was at St. Joseph's Hospital, across the street from the Disney studio, sitting bedside listening to his brother explain in exquisite detail his vision for EPCOT. Lying on his back, Walt pointed to the ceiling above him. "Now there is where the highway will run," he explained. "And there is the route for the monorail."

The next morning, Roy said goodbye at the foot of Walt's bed. He was rubbing his brother's feet, trying to keep them warm, as Walt passed into another world. Roy, eight years older than Walt, had spent his life protecting his little brother. Now he could only defend his final dream. Roy delayed retirement so he could see the company through Phase One of construction in Florida.

Walt Disney's death was worldwide news. Newspapers ran editorials and television stations ran tributes. The most eloquent eulogy came from Eric Sevareid of CBS news:

A HAPPY ACCIDENT

It would take more time than anybody has around the daily news shops to think of the right thing to say about Walt Disney.

He was an original; not just an American original, but an original, period. He was a happy accident; one of the happiest this century has experienced; and judging by the way it's been behaving in spite of all Disney tried to tell it about laughter, love, children, puppies and sunrises, the century hardly deserved him.

He probably did more to heal or at least to soothe troubled human spirits than all the psychiatrists in the world. There can't be many adults in the allegedly civilized parts of the globe who did not inhabit Disney's mind and imagination at least for a few hours and feel better for the visitation.

It may be true, as somebody said, that while there is no highbrow in a lowbrow, there is some lowbrow in every highbrow.

But what Walt Disney seemed to know was that while there is very little grown-up in a child, there is a lot of child in every grown-up. To a child this weary world is brand-new, gift wrapped; Disney tried to keep it that way for adults...

By the conventional wisdom, mighty mice, flying elephants, Snow White and Happy, Grumpy, Sneezy and Dopey—all these were fantasy, escapism from reality. It's a question of whether they are any less real, any more fantastic than intercontinental missiles, poisoned air, defoliated forests, and scraps from the moon. This is the age of fantasy, however you look at it, but Disney's fantasy wasn't lethal. People are saying we'll never see his like again.

Eric Sevareid
CBS Evening News
December 1966

"It's going to be called 'Walt Disney World' so people will always know that it was Walt's dream."

— Roy Disney

IF WALT WERE ALIVE

OUT OF ALL THE ATTRACTIONS that have come and gone at Disneyland, the one we miss the most is Walt himself. He died too young with too many dreams unfinished. He never experienced Pirates of the Caribbean (March 1967) and was dead before a spade of dirt was turned in Florida (May 1967).

We miss him.

And because we miss him so much, more than fifty years after his death, Walt Disney is as much a mythical, flawless, and fictional character as he ever was a real, flawed, human being. "If Walt were alive" is the rallying cry anytime something happens at the parks that we don't like. People presume to know exactly what Walt would think, what Walt would do, and how Walt would feel about *everything*. Yet the people who knew Walt well tell us that they *never* knew what he was going to do next. Even Walt, recognizing the distance between his public "brand" and his personal "reality," once stated: "I'm not Walt Disney. I do a lot of things that Walt Disney wouldn't do. Walt Disney doesn't smoke. I smoke. Walt Disney doesn't drink. I drink."

In his book, *Window on Main Street*, Van Arsdale France captures well the false sentiment that everything would be okay, if not perfect, if Walt were still alive. As he makes clear, it did not take long for the myths to materialize:

> Three years before this night [the night Walt died], we had engineered and built a large star which was placed by helicopter on top of the Matterhorn for the Christmas season. Now this was no ordinary star. It weighed 22 tons, and special equipment was needed to lift it to the peak of the Matterhorn. There was a highly complicated mechanism which was used for two years to make it turn, a great show. Ted Crowell was Director of Maintenance at

that time, and making that star turn was a major, expensive problem for him. It was constantly breaking down.

As the evening and the bar were both closing, Jack Sayers began to argue with Ted about the star which was supposed to turn. Ted tried to explain the problems, but Jack wouldn't listen. As I made my way out of the bar, I heard Jack say, "That star would be turning if Walt were alive!"

Jack was wrong, of course. Walt had given approval for the star *not* to be turning. That may have been the first time I heard the phrase, "if Walt were alive," but it certainly wouldn't be the last.

There is no truth to the rumor that Walt Disney was cryogenically frozen. I asked Disney Archivist Emeritus Dave Smith about this urban legend. He confirmed that Walt was cremated the day after his death and his remains are interred at Forest Lawn Cemetery in Glendale, just a few miles from where Walt worked and died in Burbank. "The rumor is very painful to the family," Smith stated.

We want to keep Walt on ice, with the prospect that he is frozen for the future, because we are unable to let him go. How does the world replace someone like Walt Disney? Van Arsdale France goes on to share the following:

On the first episode of *The Wonderful World of Color* after Walt died, no mention was made of his death. To this day some feel he is still alive.

It wasn't until four years later that Randy Bright included a segment on Walt's death in a training program. At the preview session of that program, an old studio hand became very upset. He couldn't accept that Walt was gone…even after all that time.

The morning Walt Disney died, so too did his dream for EPCOT. Walt's Experimental Prototype Community of Tomorrow became EpNOT. Phase One in Florida was always going to focus on the theme park, Magic Kingdom, along with resort hotels, a monorail-based transportation system, and other recreational activities. Then they would do EPCOT. But with Walt gone, "the EPCOT project fell apart because no one had the vision to carry it on. The whole company was lost without him."

Instead of building the City of Tomorrow, Disney folded many of Walt's ideas for his Experimental Prototype Community of Tomorrow into the Phase One construction of the Magic Kingdom. Examples include the transportation and clean energy systems, innovative construction techniques including the off-site building of completely furnished hotel rooms, a filtered tree farm, careful care for central Florida's ecosystem, a vacuum-powered trash system, and Florida's first 911 telephone system.

It is hard to lose a leader like Walt Disney and not think about what could have been. What if he had been there to finish Florida? Could he have met our expectations for EPCOT? Was Progress City even possible?

We will never know.

What I do know is that for Niki and me, Epcot is our favorite park at Walt Disney World. We never miss an opportunity to ride Spaceship Earth and have enjoyed endless evenings walking around World Showcase Lagoon, together, as we shop, drink, and eat. While enjoying Epcot, we never think about what *could* have been. We appreciate Epcot for what it *is*—our second favorite Disney park (behind Disneyland) anywhere in the world. We try to remember that "The fastest way to kill something special is to compare it to something else."

Stop asking "What if?" in your life. Accept what is, take responsibility for it, and commit to moving forward.

Walt Disney is no longer alive.

You are.

Staying stuck in yesterday isn't doing you, or anyone else, any good. Marty Sklar believed that Walt's Disney's vision for EPCOT is the example we all need for moving forward toward a better future:

> Today I believe that the creative insight that led Walt Disney to propose EPCOT is as valid as it ever was, and is needed even more than ever before.
>
> What's missing is the Walt Disney for *our* [emphasis mine] times and our challenges—the risk taker who loved to begin again and again with a new blank sheet of paper. Perhaps he was reaching for a 'Waltopia'—a utopian world of Walt's own creation. But in the words I wrote for Walt in the company's 1966 Annual Report to shareholders and employees, he expressed his creative philosophy: 'I have to move on to new things—there are many new worlds to conquer.'

What's your philosophy? What must you let go of so you can move on to a new thing? What world can you conquer when you do?

> *"The past can hurt, but the way I see it,*
> *you can either run from it or learn from it."*
>
> — Rafiki in *The Lion King*

SOUVENIR STOP

HI! MY NAME IS JEFF....

I am a big believer in counseling and support groups. I've had my share of stuff happen in life and have needed help, from time to time, letting go of past hurts, angers, disappointments, relationships, jobs, and loved ones. Let's use this Souvenir Stop to work on our *stuff*!

Before we get started, let's sit in on an actual support group! In March 2017, Mike Jacka wrote a creative article titled, "You've Got to Be Kidding: The Extinct Attractions Support Group." It is ingenious writing and provides insight into our need to let go of the past and move forward into our future.

> *We join the meeting of the Extinct Attractions Support Group as it recites the group's daily affirmation:*

> "I deserve good things. I'm entitled to provide my share of happiness. I refuse to beat myself up. I am an attractive attraction. I am a fun experience. Because I'm good enough, I'm entertaining enough, and, doggone it, Disney fans like me."

> **Therapist:** Welcome, everyone. I know most of you have attended many of our meetings. But, as always, I want to start by reminding everyone that we are here to support each other. This is an environment where all can feel safe to share. So no one is allowed to judge anyone else. No attraction is better than any other. We are all in the same boat.

> **Phantom Boats:** Is that a shot at me?!

> **Therapist:** I'm sorry, Phantom. That was a poor choice of words. As the very first extinct attraction, you are a valuable asset—someone we can lean on to better understand what it really means to be an extinct attraction.

Phantom Boats: That's okay. It's just that it's been such a long, long time. It wears on me and.... No. Wait. There's something I've been wanting to get off my chest. You always say we should feel safe to share, right?

Therapist: Go ahead, Phantom. What is it?

Phantom Boats: It's just that...well...I've never understood why you let *them* in here!

Country Bear Jamboree, PeopleMover, and Carousel of Progress all glare back at Phantom Boats' pointing finger.

Country Bear Jamboree: Now hold on there. I don't have to sit here and listen to this chit chat, yick yack, and flim flam. Just because our cousins in Florida are still around doesn't mean we are any less extinct. Why, if I had a ladder....

Therapist: Everyone calm down. Every park has its own extinct attractions. The Anaheim Chapter of the Extinct Attractions Support Group is not alone. There are chapters in Orlando, Paris, and Japan. In fact, chapters are already being formed in Hong Kong and Shanghai. This isn't about judging the extinctness of any attraction. This is about helping each other. So let's not fight now. We've got work to do.

You get the idea. Here is a link to the full article: http://micechat. com/154733-youve-got-kidding-extinct-attractions-support-group/

Inspired by the idea that "We've got work to do," let's explore the following:

LISTEN TO "LET IT GO"—WITH 1.3 billion in box office revenue, the 2013 movie *Frozen* is the number one animated feature film of all time. Why? Because everyone wants what Elsa wants—happiness, freedom, with no one interfering.

"Let It Go," a song from the soundtrack, is as popular as the picture. As you listen to the song ask yourself these questions:

1. What must you let go of so you can grow up and move on?

_____

_____

2. What must you let go of so you can become your own person?

_____

_____

3. What must you let go of so you can be yourself—no longer ashamed of who you really are? _____

_____

_____

DO YOU WANT TO BUILD a Snowman?—Often action, any action, is the solution to getting unstuck. Regardless of what you are struggling to let go of, pick a project, any project, that you can start working on *today*! Stop thinking and start doing. Before you know it, your mind will be elsewhere and you will have jump-started the process of *letting it go*!

START A NEW STORY—EVERY ATTRACTION at a Disney park tells a story. Replacing an old attraction means the start of a new story. For example, Epcot recently replaced the Maelstrom attraction in the Norway Pavilion with Frozen Ever After. The attraction is in the same pavilion and uses the same boats and the same track as the old. The story, however, is completely different.

You can do the same. The life my wife, Niki, and I live today looks *nothing* like the life we lived a decade ago. We are still the same people, housed in the same bodies, but we made the decision to let go of our past and start living a better, brighter story. We aren't perfect, and we still have stuff to work on, especially me, but we couldn't possibly be happier.

GETTING YOUR HAND STAMPED

When Walt Disney opened Disneyland, he wanted to do everything differently, including operating hours. Rather than only open seasonally, with an ever-changing shift of seasonal workers, Walt created his park with a family of cast members whom he kept employed and engaged throughout the year. A year-round amusement park? Crazy!

Twenty-two thousand (and counting) operating days later, Disneyland has experienced only two unscheduled closings. The first came the day after President Kennedy's assassination in 1963. The second closing came on September 11, 2001 in response to the terrorist attacks—the only closing shared by both Disneyland in California and Walt Disney World in Florida.

There was nearly a third.

When Walt Disney died at 9:35 a.m. on December 15, 1966, a serious struggle ensued within the company about what to do with Disneyland that day. With opening less than thirty minutes away, they had to make a quick decision: "Should we open or stay closed?" This was the first of many, "What would Walt do?" questions that Disney executives would ask over the next several years.

Many presumed the park would remain closed "in order to honor Walt." Disney did the opposite. The *best* way to honor Walt was to keep his beloved Disneyland open for the people he loved most—the public. Disney demurred to Lillian and Roy; both believed that Walt would want "the show to go on." Dick Nunis rationalized the decision this way: "Walt was always about doing right by the people. People have driven here to come to the park, and they are going to have a park to enjoy."

Nonetheless, it was a solemn day inside "The Happiest Place on Earth." Cast members lowered the flag to half-staff, and many were seen crying off and on throughout the day. Pat Williams and Jim Denney describe the day further:

> The day Walt died was chilly and gray in southern California. All of Orange County was in the grip of an icy cold snap. The air over Disneyland was heavy with a damp, mournful fog. Late that afternoon, an announcer's voice came over the loudspeakers throughout the park, telling visitors what most of them already knew: Walt Disney had died that day. At Town Square, the Disneyland band played "When You Wish Upon a Star."

> As dusk settled over the park, Disneyland cast member Don Payne was in a character costume, waiting with dozens of co-workers on the service road behind the Main Street firehouse gate. In moments, they would begin the premiere performance of the 1966 Disneyland Christmas Parade.

> It was Don's eighteenth birthday, and for days he had been hoping that Walt would be there, perhaps in his apartment over the firehouse, watching the debut of the new parade. But as Don looked up at Walt's empty apartment, he felt only a disappointed sadness.

> Grief wrapped the parade like a funeral pall. Ahead of Don, a female cast member pointed skyward. "Look!" she said. "It's snowing!" A soft sprinkling of snowflakes drifted from the sky, sparkling in the glare of a floodlight atop the Main

Street Emporium. The delicate crystals melted instantly on contact with the ground.

Why did it snow at Disneyland, a rare sight in Southern California, the night Walt Disney died? I can give you the meteorological explanation—something to do with water, clouds, cold fronts, and temperatures—but that's not what matters. The real answer rests inside the park's nightly fireworks.

To "pluss" the show ("pluss" and "plussing" were Walt-created words), Disneyland's fireworks began bursting over Sleeping Beauty Castle during the summer of 1958. Always state of the art, they symbolize the closing of the curtain on the day's fun. For Walt, the fireworks were his "kiss goodnight" to guests as they exited the park and headed home.

Now Walt was gone. The curtain on his life had closed. He, too, had headed home.

I believe the snow was Walt Disney's kiss *goodbye*. And a magical reminder, right there on Main Street, of one of life's most important lessons: The show must go on.

"He affects all of us.
No one is untouched by Walt Disney."

— PBS documentary,
The American Experience: Walt Disney

CHOOSING TO CHANGE

*"Times and conditions change so rapidly that we must
keep our aim constantly focused on the future."*

— Walt Disney

WHERE'S EPCOT?

AFTER WALT'S DEATH, THE DISNEY company experienced significant change with the most immediate being Walt's dream for EPCOT. Without Walt, the dreamer and visionary, the company was no longer interested in building and managing a futuristic city. Nonetheless, it was committed to Florida, and the State had granted it huge governmental concessions in exchange for building EPCOT. After the Magic Kingdom opened in October 1971, to rave reviews, it wasn't long before people started asking, "Where's EPCOT?" Jeff Kurti describes the dilemma best:

> Walt's creative heirs, continually being judged by the media and the public, suffered a great dilemma. They could carry forth with an urban development project of gargantuan proportions (a project that faced the very real possibility of conceptual failure, corporate embarrassment, and a complete drain on the company's funds) or face the slings

and arrows that would come with their perceived failure to carry out Walt's last great dream. In the end, compromise was inevitable, and the solution was relatively simple: the concepts and ideals embodied in Walt's best intentions for his model city could be folded into a new take on one of Disney's great strengths—the theme park.

During the 1970s, Disney worked on creating multiple parks that would embody the best of what Walt wanted in EPCOT. One would focus on the future, the other on showcasing countries and cultures from around the world. Both parks required significant sponsorship, but the global economy in the 1970s made it impossible for Disney to find enough participants for two parks. To make Epcot a reality, another change was necessary. Marty Sklar shared what happened next:

> Facing the dilemma of not enough industry sponsors for Epcot's Future World, or international participation in the World Showcase, John Hench and I made a major design decision, literally, about one hour before a key meeting with the Studio brass. With the help of our Model Shop staff, we pushed the project models for Future World and World Showcase together—creating one project with enough potential participants combined to provide the seed money that suggested the sales effort could be a success. Imagineering's model makers set a new record for patching and painting the two models into one complete idea, making it look as though it had been designed that way, and not slapped together in a matter of minutes.

Change is never easy but always inevitable. When I was five years old, my mother changed the red-and-white checked curtains in our kitchen. I cried for days. The fact that I am writing about it more than forty-five years later tells you that I am *still* not over it. So much for learning to let things go....

This is how some Disney fans feel about Walt's vision for EPCOT. They've never forgiven the company for changing the dream of an Experimental Prototype Community of Tomorrow into just another theme park. But even before Walt died, EPCOT was *already* changing. Walt Disney's final film was a promotional video for EPCOT that he recorded less than two months before his death. In the movie, Walt cautions us that, "[T]he sketches and plans you will see today are simply a starting point; everything in this room may change time and time again as we move ahead." Even before his death, Walt altered the plans from including permanent residents to temporary residents—a necessary adjustment if he was going to keep the control he craved.

Even building Epcot as a theme park required Disney to change. More than thirty-five years after its opening, we forget what a radical concept Epcot was even as a theme park, as explained by the website Theme Park Insider:

> Consider what a tremendous shift the very concept represented. After all, at this time in Disney history, there were only two 'Disney parks' in the world: the original Disneyland and its younger sister, Magic Kingdom. That meant that for millions upon millions of American families who'd visited "Disney" or dreamed of doing so, "Disney" was synonymous with castles, fairytale lands, princesses, and meeting beloved Disney characters straight from animated films.
>
> EPCOT Center would be different. It would be a living showcase of corporate innovation, emerging technologies, cultural stories, and the true tales behind science and

industry. No princesses. No characters. No movies. No *Mickey*.

No Mickey? That's right! Epcot was such a change for Disney that it made the dramatic decision to exclude Mickey Mouse and the gang from Walt Disney World's second theme park. Executives, thinking that Mickey and Minnie wouldn't mix well with the availability of alcohol and the more adult-oriented nature of the new park, proclaimed that the beloved Disney characters would *never* be seen in Epcot. Imagineers, remembering that Walt once said, "I only hope that we don't lose sight of one thing—that it was all started by a mouse," took up the challenge. They began "hiding" Mickey's simple, three-circle profile in their designs throughout the park—giving birth to today's popular hunts for "Hidden Mickeys" around the world.

Think about where you are. Think about where you want to be. Now think about the changes you know you need to make to get there. Some of them are obvious while others might be hidden. Either way, the first choice you must make is to believe—to believe that change is possible and to know that where you are heading already exists. Walt promised that EPCOT would "always be in a state of becoming." Disney is honoring this vision. While I was writing this book, the company announced that $2 billion dollars' worth of changes and upgrades are coming to Epcot. You and I need to make the same promise to ourselves—always be changing so you can always be in a state of becoming.

The world Niki and I currently inhabit did not exist nine years ago. At least not in the physical world. We had a vision for what our life together could be, so we set out to make the difficult but necessary changes to create that reality. We believe that life is a story, complete with a soundtrack, and for us, no band has been more instrumental than Sister Hazel, a group out of Gainesville, Florida. Recently, we had the privilege of meeting the band members before a show in Anaheim, so we shared with them our story. Our conversation with lead singer

Ken Block centered on our shared belief that you can change the world by changing your mind—which is why he wrote the hit song "Change Your Mind."

> *If you want to be somebody else,*
> *If you're tired of fighting battles with yourself*
> *If you want to be somebody else*
> *Change your mind*

NEW HORIZONS

No attraction in Disney history gave guests more choice than Horizons in Epcot's Future World. This show, sponsored by General Electric and created as the "sequel" to the beloved Carousel of Progress, opened on Epcot's one-year anniversary. The other Future World pavilions represented the oceans, the environments, the imagination, energy, innovation, and communication. Horizons, however, tied every element together and showed the future from the perspective of one American family.

The building looked like a spaceship, and guests, four at a time, rode in Omnimover vehicles via an overhead track—a Haunted Mansion meets Peter Pan kind of experience. The first part of the fifteen-minute journey gave guests a look at "past" visions of the future. Moving forward, guests then chose from three possible destinations: Nova Cite—an urban center in space; Mesa Verde—a desert farming community; or Sea Castle—an underwater city.

Today, Mission Space sits where Horizons once stood. Nonetheless, older guests remember it fondly as "the greatest ride in Epcot history." Horizons is also where guests first heard, "If you can dream it, you can do it." Words that we, myself included, often attribute to Walt.

As we think about our own horizon, let's use the original Horizons attraction experience to explore three kinds of choices we must make on our way to success. Those three choices are:

1. Reimagine Reality
2. Take Decisive Action
3. Create More Capacity

"If you can dream it, you can do it," is true, but only when you choose to make these three choices. Let's examine each choice in the sections below.

1. REIMAGINE REALITY
WHAT AN AMUSEMENT PARK SHOULD BE

DESPITE HIS DESIRE TO BUILD a theme park rather than an amusement park, Walt analyzed the amusement park industry in advance of designing Disneyland. Sites studied included nearby Knott's Berry Farm, cross-country Coney Island, and Tivoli Gardens in distant Denmark. The only enterprise close to what Walt envisioned was Tivoli Gardens. According to Sam Gennawey in *The Disneyland* Story, Walt was attracted to the park's popcorn lighting, cleanliness, outdoor entertainment, pricing, orderly layout with plenty of places to sit and relax, its appeal to children and adults, and the absence of alcohol and raucous entertainment. During his visit to Tivoli Gardens in 1951, Walt turned to Lillian at the end of the evening and said, "Now, this is what an amusement park should be."

Analysis of other parks all but ended in 1953 after Walt sent three employees and two consultants to Chicago for a convention of the National Association of Parks, Pools, and Beaches. At the end of the week, the team from Disney persuaded seven amusement park industry experts to an evening presentation on the overall concept of Disneyland.

They hated it.

Disneyland would cost too much to build and maintain. As a single entrance, Main Street, U.S.A. was too much of a bottleneck. Too much lavish landscaping. Too many sit-down restaurants. Too many attractions such as the castle and a pirate ship that produced zero revenue. Not nearly enough rides. And they especially hated Walt's plan to charge for admission and then sell individual tickets for the various shows and attractions.

Their dismay convinced Walt that he was on the right track. What the "experts" missed was that Disneyland wasn't about rides. The park was the attraction—a show that Walt believed would sell itself. It would attract guests to his new form of outdoor entertainment. Charging admission into an amusement park was unheard of in 1955, but according to Jack Lindquist, "[T]hat is just what Walt wanted. He needed to make a statement that Disneyland was not an amusement park; it was a totally new experience designed to entertain people of all ages in an entirely new environment."

A totally new environment. A totally new experience. Sit for a moment and soak that in for a second. How amazing does that feel?

When you set out to change the world, you first may need to change *your* world. Love it or hate it, you created your current reality. It is a byproduct of your past and current thinking, choices, and actions. Your life story has a theme. Like the attractions that lure guests into the parks, you invite your environment and experiences. Looking for a change? Something new? Something different? Then reimagine your reality!

"Live life by a theme instead of a goal."

— James Altucher

THIS IS REALITY

Choosing to change EPCOT from an experimental city to a theme park allowed Disney to leverage its proven strength in creating outdoor, themed entertainment environments. But building Epcot as a theme park rather than a city begs the question: What exactly *is* a Disney park?

While it was apparent in 1955 that Disneyland was *not* an amusement park, that didn't mean that Walt had a better word for explaining his new world. Eventually, the term "theme park" developed. What's the difference? In *Persistence of Vision* magazine, J.G. O'Boyle tells us that "[A] theme park is not ride-dependent. A theme park without rides is still a theme park. An amusement park without rides is a parking lot with popcorn."

I understand this now more than ever.

In *The Wisdom of Walt*, I wrote about being diagnosed with a brain tumor the day after giving the first lecture in my dream class "The History of Disneyland." My neurosurgeon urged immediate surgery, but I took the risk of delaying the procedure, for two-and-a-half months so I could finish the class. At the post-operative exam, Niki and I learned that the tumor was not cancerous. Yay! We also learned that I was grounded from most amusement park rides, Disney or otherwise, for two years. Boo!

Did this mean we stopped going to Disneyland? Of course not! Sure, I missed my favorite attractions, especially Space Mountain. The wait was worse when Disney converted its cosmic adventure into Hyperspace Mountain. Hyperspace Mountain was scheduled to run from November 2014 through May 2015, meaning I would miss it entirely. When I complained about this to my daughter, Bethany, she unsympathetically replied, "Well, you know, Dad, if you had gone ahead with the surgery when you were supposed to...."

Fortunately, the overlay was so popular that Disney extended the original schedule and I did get to experience it, at long last, at 8:13 a.m. on Sunday, July 24, 2016—exactly two years after my successful surgery. In the interim, Niki and I kept returning to the parks like always. Why?

Remember the Dr. Seuss cartoon, *How the Grinch Stole Christmas*? (By the way, the song "You're a Mean One, Mr. Grinch" was sung by Disney legend Thurl Ravenscroft.) In that classic Christmas special, the Grinch mistakes Christmas as being about the gifts, the presents, the toys, and the tinsel. After he succeeds in stealing everything that he thinks is "Christmas," he is shocked to discover that the Whos of

Whoville wake up on Christmas Day and gather together to celebrate and sing—regardless.

The same is true at Disneyland and Walt Disney World. Take out every "ride," which is what I experienced for two years, and people will still come. Disneyland is not an escape; it is an example. Walt Disney World isn't the place where "dreams come true." It is *showing* us how to make our own dreams come true. Perhaps architect Robert Venturi summed it up best when he said, "Disney World is nearer to what people really want than anything architects have ever given them."

Walt Disney loved giving tours of Disneyland. One of my favorite stories comes from when he was giving a tour to Evangelist Billy Graham. While walking through the park, Graham gave Walt what he thought was a compliment: "This is a nice fantasy you have created." Instead of soaking in the praise, Walt was stunned and incensed. He turned to Graham and told him, pointedly, "You know the fantasy isn't here. This is very real.... The Park is reality. The people are natural here; they're having a good time; they're communicating. This is what people really are. The fantasy is—out there, outside the gates of Disneyland, where people have hatreds and people have prejudices. It's not really real!"

Is it possible for people to create their own realities? Walt Disney did with Disneyland. Others throughout history support the same thoughts. Regardless of your faith, you will find words of wisdom below:

Jesus: "It is done unto you as you believe." (Matthew 8:13)

Jewish Talmud: "We do not see things as they are; we see them as we are."

Buddha: "What you dwell upon you become."

Hindu: "Whatever a person's mind dwells on intensely and with firm resolve, that is exactly what he becomes."

What do you want your reality to be? You know you need to make changes, but you also need to know where those changes will take you. Walt Disney imagined the reality of Space Mountain, a roller-coaster ride in the dark, a decade before the technology existed to make the ride a reality. Imagineer John Hench loved the concept so much that he built a model of Space Mountain and kept it beside him, on his desk, for ten years while he waited for the technology to come along. Finally, it was built first for Florida in 1975 and then Disneyland in 1977. Can you imagine a Disney park today without Space Mountain?

Exactly.

"We are whatever we pretend to be."

— Kurt Vonnegut

2. TAKE DECISIVE ACTION
DISNEYLAND IS GOOD FOR YOU

ONE OF THE REASONS WE don't change is because life already feels overwhelming and the various choices about what to change, and how, can be even more overwhelming. It is human nature to avoid both conflict and chaos. Why not just escape and head to Walt Disney World instead?

Except that the parks aren't about escape. They're about reassurance. The reassurance that everything can be okay. That life is good. We can win at conflict, eliminate chaos, and change our world into that new reality we have already imagined.

One of the good things about living in the twenty-first century is that we live in the "Information Age." Information is good, but only to a point. Living the life you desire requires you to lead yourself in your newfound direction, and leadership is about taking charge and making decisions. Too many of us, however, do analysis to the point of paralysis and remain stuck because we can't decide.

In an article dated December 4, 1978, titled "Disneyland Is Good for You," by Charlie Haas of *New West* magazine, John Hench discusses the reassurance we feel when we make our way through the Magic Kingdom. Part of the reason why we feel better, and we know that life can be good again, is because Disney assists with our decision-making by giving us fewer choices:

> If you're at a state fair or something, everything clamors for you, so you look and you look and you try to make sense out of things, you try to decide and you constantly make a lot of judgments. But here, when we come to a point in the park that we know is a decision point, we put two choices. We try not to give them seven or eight so that they have to decide in a qualitative way which is the best of those. You just give them two. Then we get the guy farther along and he has another choice, but we're not giving him four to begin with. We unfold these things, so that they're normal.

Life is full of decision points, and none of us wants to make a mistake. But not deciding *is* a decision—a decision to stay exactly where you already are—which can be the biggest mistake of all.

Choosing to change is a courageous choice. Sometimes we make our decisions way more complicated than they need to be simply to avoid changing. In *Start: Punch Fear in the Face, Escape Average and Do Work that Matters*, Jon Acuff illustrates this well in the following story:

> My friend Tim in Atlanta often misses breakfast meetings. He doesn't want to. He is actually one of the kindest, most conscientious people I've ever met. He sends handwritten

thank-you notes after he eats dinner at our house, the kind of notes that my wife holds up and says, "See? See? This is how to be a gentleman."

But he has a hard time getting to breakfast on time or at all. One time it was because his iPhone battery was dead and its alarm didn't go off. Another morning it was because his iPhone was in another room and he didn't hear it. Another morning it was because he had the sound turned down too low and he didn't hear it. And still another morning it was because...well, you get the picture.

The solution to this dilemma is not very difficult. It is not complex. One must not call a brain storming meeting to hash out possible fixes. The solution is a $10 alarm clock. It couldn't be simpler. It automatically fixes all the issues he's had with his iPhone alarm. So why didn't Tim just fix the problem with the simple solution the first time his iPhone clock plan failed?

Because we love complex problems and are terrified of simple solutions. We tend to add complexities to our challenges because if the problem is simple to solve, then we have to change. And change is scary. So when faced with a challenge we really don't want to fix, we tend to overcomplicate the issues. We blame our iPhones for not waking us up. What did we even do before we had cell phones with alarm clocks?

I am often asked how long it took me to write my first book, *The Wisdom of Walt*. My answer is always "Twenty years and 142 days... and the only part that matters is the 142 days." The idea for the book came to me in the early 1990s. I spent two decades thinking about it, dreaming about it, but unable to make a meaningful decision about it. It took getting sick in 2014 for me finally to get serious about it. Once recovered, I knew it was now or never, and Niki and I chose *now*. Once we made that decision, what had previously been delayed for more than two decades was completed in fewer than five months.

The best way to whittle down your options is to focus on what you want based on what you value. Roy Disney once said, "[I]t's not hard to make decisions once you know what your values are." Think about what *you* value and what decisions you need to make *today* that reflect the values of the world you are working to create. While you think about that, I want to share a story from Epcot that again illustrates the importance of limiting our options and taking decisive action.

One of the biggest challenges in getting Epcot constructed was the need for corporate sponsors to join with Disney in presenting the various shows and attractions. This led to many meetings with industry and company leaders, usually CEOs who held the various reins of power and inevitably made the final decisions. In his book, *Dream It! Do It!*, Marty Sklar noted that many of those meetings were memorable, not only because so much was riding on each potential agreement, but also because of the quirkiness of some of those lauded leaders.

My favorite CEO story comes from Harry Gray, the head of United Technologies and sponsor of the Living Seas Pavilion in Future World. Today, The Living Seas Pavilion is home to Nemo and Friends, but when it was first constructed, it was noted for being the world's largest oceanic environment ever built (5.7 million gallons of water) *and* for the use of ozone rather than chlorine. What was memorable for Marty, however, was Gray's insistence on painting the exterior of the pavilion bright white.

John Hench, the same Imagineer who once insisted on the entire repainting of Main Street in Florida's Magic Kingdom because of the difference in the effects of the sun in Florida versus California, and "one of the most knowledgeable designers in the world on the theory and effect of color, visually and emotionally," did not think this was a bright idea at all. His rationale was that the fearsome Florida sun against a bright white building would inevitably blind the Epcot guests. It was clear, however, that Gray was in charge and would not be easily swayed by a mere Imagineer. Hench then decided that a demonstration was in order, giving Gray the opportunity to pick which shade of white should be used.

On the day of the demonstration, a bright and sunny afternoon, Harry Gray arrived with his wife, Helen. Hench lined up the painters and challenged Gray to select from the thirty-four shades of white used in Disney parks (there is a *Fifty Shades of Gray* joke here; I just don't know what it is.)

Thirty-four shades? Thirty-four? I *might* be able to choose from three. Give me thirty-four choices of anything and I will never decide.

And neither will you.

Decisive action means limiting your options, deciding quickly on one, and then going for it with everything you've got. Don't overcomplicate things because change is already hard enough.

By the way, Harry Gray couldn't decide either. Just before the demonstration, his wife, Helen, pulled Marty Sklar aside: "Marty, why are you asking Harry about color? I pick out his ties every morning because he's color blind."

> *"Many executives in Hollywood agonize over decisions. My experience is that ideas don't get better or worse over time, and success depends not just on having good creative instincts but on the willingness to act on them quickly and decisively. My confidence came from knowing what I liked and discovering, over the years, that I was right often enough that it made up for the many times when I proved to be wrong."*
>
> — Michael Eisner

3. CREATE MORE CAPACITY
A YO HO LIFE

AFTER OVERCOMING THE OVERWHELMING OBSTACLES he faced in both financing and finishing the park, and facing the real challenges of Disneyland's opening day, known infamously as "Black Sunday," Walt faced a brand-new challenge.

Success.

You wouldn't think that success could be a challenge, but it often is. That is exactly what Walt experienced in 1955 and what Walt Disney World experienced again in 1971. With attendance at Disneyland during its first summer running 50 percent higher than the most optimistic projections, Walt had to figure out a way to increase capacity as quickly as possible.

When it comes to capacity, we humans are interesting creatures. If we find a line that is too long, then we will give up and move on. If, however, we find a line that is empty, then we presume there is nothing of interest, so we will also move along. Given that the continued success of the park was dependent on guests buying tickets for the individual attractions, Walt found himself in the role of Goldilocks—he needed to keep the number of attractions, and the ensuing lines, "just right."

Walt got busy working to find attractions that could add capacity and shorten the lines. According to Stephanie Barczewski in *Magic Kingdoms: A History of Disney Theme Parks*, the Astro-Jets in Tomorrowland, which premiered on April 2, 1956, "holds a place in Disneyland history as the first major new ride to be added after opening day." The beloved *Skyway* that transported guests from Fantasyland to Tomorrowland, and back again, along with the opening of Tom Sawyer Island, followed a few months later during Disneyland's first full summer.

Many see Pirates of the Caribbean at Disneyland as the "world's greatest theme park attraction." The Florida version, despite all the extra land at Walt Disney World, is significantly shorter, not nearly as popular, and doesn't come close to manifesting the same magic as the original. Imagineer and Disney Legend Tony Baxter explains further in David Koenig's *Realityland*:

> The Pirate ride in Florida has never garnered the same mystique as the one in California. And I'm convinced that there's a level of removal that goes on as you descend deeper and deeper into this dreamlike state where finally at the last, lowest level it all comes to life. The characters are there, alive and so forth. In Florida you just put your packages away, you cast off, and—boom—you're in the city. Then, while you're still in there, struggling with the pirates and the prison, you hear the girl on the intercom saying, 'Ladies and gentlemen, please stand and exit to your right.' It's rather jarring to be asked to leave when there are people dying in the cell next to you. So I don't think it's ever connected. And the romance of the Blue Bayou is gone and all those things that really help to set this one up. I think the lesson learned in Florida was you can't race people into something, whether it's a queue line or it's a conditioning experience.

Pirates in Florida is, in fact, a "success" if you judge it by the main purpose for which it was built. It has a capacity of 4,300 guests per hour. A capacity that was desperately needed in 1973 due to the growing popularity of Walt Disney World's Magic Kingdom.

When Epcot eventually opened on October 1, 1982, exactly eleven years after the opening of Walt Disney World, Disney *needed* it to be a theme park. The success of the Magic Kingdom, the East Coast Disneyland, meant that the park was often at capacity with guests clamoring for more. Opening a second park would, hopefully, relieve the relentless pressure on the Magic Kingdom. Epcot did exactly that, and more. Executives estimated that attendance would jump from more than twelve million guests the previous year to eighteen million during Epcot's inaugural year. Twenty-four million came instead.

Epcot's expansive size—it is more than double the size of the Magic Kingdom and can hold *both* California parks—handled everyone with ease. As you start to make your own changes and begin moving forward to your new reality, you must also be prepared for the success these changes will bring. Many of us prepare for failure, but few realize they need to prepare for success as well.

In his book, *The Big Leap: Conquer Your Hidden Fear and Take Life to the Next Level*, Gay Hendricks writes about the *Upper Limit Problem*. Hendricks believes that "each of us has an inner thermostat [capacity] setting that determines how much love, success, and creativity we allow ourselves to enjoy. When we exceed our inner thermostat setting, we will often do something to sabotage ourselves, causing us to drop back into the old, familiar zone where we feel secure."

Taking your life and your success to the next level means increasing your current capacity for success—another change you must choose to make. Making this change means making the choice to enjoy what you have right now and believing that you can continue to enjoy your success as you expand into an even greater future. Hendricks writes further:

Your capacity expands in small increments each time you consciously let yourself enjoy the money you have, the love you feel, and the creativity you are expressing in the world. As that capacity for enjoyment expands, so does your financial abundance, the love you feel, and the creativity you express....

If you focus for a moment, you can always find some place in you that feels good right now. Your task is to give the expanding positive feeling your full attention. When you do, you will find that it expands with your attention. Let yourself enjoy it as long as you possibly can.

One of my favorite "increasing capacity" stories comes from Disneyland's earliest days. As the park struggled with its success, someone came up with an ingenious way of increasing capacity without taking the time, or the expense, of creating an entirely new attraction. The Jungle Cruise has always been popular, and *overnight*, Disneyland was able to increase capacity, with an attraction it already had, by 40 percent by cutting the canopy so guests could load in both the front *and* rear of the boat.

What do you already have that makes you grateful? How can you leverage that today so you can increase your capacity for success tomorrow? Don't be like the fellow Disney author I met at a book signing who was disappointed at the end of the day because he only sold thirty-five books. Then he admitted that he *only* brought thirty-five books. Be prepared for success!

SOUVENIR STOP

A FIGMENT OF YOUR IMAGINATION—WITH the decision to exclude Mickey Mouse from Epcot, Disney designed a new character, Figment, for the Imagination Pavilion. Guests missed Mickey, but Figment quickly became a fan favorite. He is an impish, purple dragon sidekick to the lead character, Dreamfinder, with "a one-second attention span and unbridled enthusiasm."

According to Figment's creator, Tony Baxter, everyone was familiar with the phrase "figment of the imagination," but no one had ever seen a figment. "No one had ever visualized it. No one had ever drawn what a figment looks like. So, here is a word that already has a great meaning to people but no one has ever seen it! I had discovered a name that was just waiting for us to give it life and a personality as a partner to Dreamfinder."

Use the space below to find your dream. Use the "figments of your imagination" to write out in as much detail as possible what your reimagined world will look like.

_____

_____

_____

_____

*"You are creating the reality you are experiencing
right now in your life and in your career."*

— Mindy Mackenzie

LET YOUR HEART DECIDE—IMAGINE SPENDING your day at Walt Disney World unable to decide which park to visit, which attraction to experience, which show to see, or which food to eat. For many of us, this is far too close to real life to feel anything like a vacation!

What decision have you been delaying for days, weeks, months, or even years? Rather than focusing on all your options, use the space below to write down what you value in relation to the decision you need to make.

_____

_____

_____

_____

One of the fastest decisions Michael Eisner ever made was green lighting the concept for Walt Disney World's second water park, Blizzard Beach. A water park in Florida built around a freak snowstorm that had since melted was a "no-brainer."

Summit Plummet is the signature attraction at Blizzard Beach. It is twelve stories tall with a sheer 120-foot drop. The park opens each morning with guests doing a five-second countdown for the first rider taking the first plunge. Limit your options to two and then give yourself five seconds to let your heart decide and take the plunge: 5, 4, 3, 2, 1!

Now, go take decisive action with the reassurance that you can always change and make a different decision. You can also rest in the reassurance that bad decisions always make for the best stories.

"When you spend less time deciding, you conserve energy and accomplish more things."

— Stephen Guise

A TICKET TO RIDE—TO HELP manage capacity, and the misconception that Disneyland cost too much, Walt introduced the famous Disneyland ticket books in October 1955. The system was so successful, and so famous, that Disney employed it again when it opened the Magic Kingdom in Florida in 1971.

Whatever happened to the ticket books? Epcot happened. As a theme park that focused far more on shops and restaurants than rides, Disney was never going to get its $1.2 billion-dollar investment back by selling A-E coupons. Plus, how do you tell a country in World Showcase that it is only an "A" ticket while the rival country next door is an "E"? Thus, Disney decided to change its ticketing structure in 1982 by eliminating the coupon books and introducing the all-inclusive ticket. All the other Disney parks changed as well.

What is your ticket to success? Use the space below to write down the five changes you know you must make in the next thirty days to increase your current and future capacity for success. When it comes to creating more capacity in your life, be sure to go to the end of the row and fill in all the available seats!

1. _____

2. _____

3. _____

4. _____

5. _____

GETTING YOUR HAND STAMPED

FOR NEARLY THIRTY YEARS, DISNEY didn't do any advertising for its theme parks. It didn't need to. Guests came away from a day at Disneyland or Walt Disney World so enamored with their experience that they happily shared their stories with friends and neighbors who soon found themselves planning their own theme park vacation. This free publicity, coupled with free stories in the press by reporters who routinely covered the parks during the opening of a new attraction or anniversary celebration, was enough to attract guests to Disney and keep the turnstiles moving.

In 1984, Michael Eisner (Chairman and Chief Executive Officer) and Frank Wells (President) arrived with an aggressive attitude and no limits on what could or could not be done. They wanted to market the parks more effectively. Not a terribly difficult task considering almost no marketing had been done previously. Tom Elrod, Walt Disney World's marketing chief, explained to Eisner, "You can see how much we've accomplished without advertising. Just think what wonders we could do with it."

A few years later, and because of a willingness to change, Disney developed one of the most memorable advertising campaigns of all-time. Eisner explains further in his book *Work in Progress*:

> No campaign we undertook achieved more visibility than our "What's Next?" ads. Early in 1987, Frank and I had a dinner inside Disneyland with George Lucas and several celebrities we'd invited to promote the opening of *Star Tours*, among them Jeana Yeager and Dick Rutan. The couple had made headlines a month earlier by piloting a single-engine plane around the world on one tank of gas.

At some point in the evening, my wife turned to Rutan, "Now that you've flown around the world and done the most adventurous thing imaginable," Jane asked reasonably enough, "what are you going to do next?"

"Well, we're going to Disneyland," he replied sincerely. As soon as she had a chance, Jane pulled me aside and described the exchange. "This would make a great advertising campaign," she said. By the middle of the night I was addicted to the idea. The next morning, I called Tom Elrod. Two weeks later [talk about decisive action!], at the Super Bowl in Pasadena, the New York Giants overwhelmed the Denver Broncos. As the Giants quarterback walked to the sidelines, he stopped for the camera crew we had waiting. "Phil Simms, you've just won the Super Bowl," an off-camera voice asks. "What are you going to do next?" He looked at the camera with a big smile and replied, "I'm going to Disneyland." We had arranged for Simms to spend the next day at the park with his wife and young children, appearing in our parades, taking his kids on rides, and making a slew of media appearances— each using Disneyland as a backdrop.

To our amazement, the campaign acquired a certain icon status. World-famous athletes were suddenly eager to have the "What's Next?" ad on their resumes. At major sports events, we would typically make provisional deals with each of the athletes most likely to emerge as the game's standout. During the past decade, we've produced dozens of spots at major events. We've used the campaign not just to honor athletes ranging from John Elway to Michael Jordan but to celebrate others who've achieved something outstanding. The campaign has given our parks and the company enormous visibility, but it also has a subtler effect: powerfully identifying Disney with excitement and achievement, triumph and joy.

Today, asking someone "What are you going to do next?" is a part of the American cultural lexicon. And it's not just for Super Bowl champions or *American Idol* winners. What will *you* do next? Anything is possible, but it takes more than just wishing upon a star and hoping for the best.

Make the choice to change. Know that you can renegotiate your current reality. Start taking decisive action and create a greater capacity for *your* success.

What are Niki and I doing when I finish *Beyond the Wisdom of Walt*? We are going to Disney World!

And we look forward to seeing you there.

> *"Human beings follow through on*
> *who they believe they are."*
>
> — Tony Robbins

LEADING YOURSELF

"I give myself very good advice, but I very seldom follow it."

— Alice in *Alice in Wonderland*

THE BUCK STOPS HERE

Harry S. Truman led the free world as the United States' thirty-third president. He is remembered as "Give 'em Hell, Harry," a slogan born from his unflinching lack of fear in speaking the truth and for taking full responsibility via his famous desk sign, "The Buck Stops Here." What Truman most wanted to stop was the threat of communism, and he was the first US president to face off against the Soviet Union during the Cold War. A few years after leaving the White House, Harry and his wife, Bess, wanted to go where every other American wanted to go in the 1950s—Disneyland. The famous couple made their famed visit in 1957. Jack Lindquist—also a president—president of Disneyland, remembers Truman, despite the entourage of secret service, photographers, and reporters, as "just so ordinary and nice."

The most memorable moment from that visit took place in Fantasyland. According to Lindquist—and contrary to almost every other story about this scene—as soon as Truman saw the Dumbo ride he declared, "I want to go on that!" Bess, remembering that the elephant was the eternal symbol of the rival Republican Party, wondered out loud whether Harry had lost his mind. "That's a Republican elephant. The press will have a field day with you riding on a GOP (Grand Old Party) symbol."

"No, it's *not* a Republican elephant. It's Dumbo!" Harry replied.

"Harry!" Bess implored.

"Bess, I don't give a damn" was Truman's retort.

Truman took his turn on Dumbo, and sure enough, newspapers across the country ran pictures of the former Democratic president enjoying himself at Disneyland, but most symbolically, taking a spin on an elephant. "This guy was real," says Lindquist. "He didn't care what others thought."

President Truman may have been a politician, but when it came to leadership, he was certainly no Dumbo. We see this in his ability to speak the truth and his willingness to take responsibility for his decisions, his actions, and his results. Truman took to heart the truism that if you wish to lead others, then you first must learn to lead yourself.

> *"To be able to lead others, a man*
> *must be willing to go forward alone."*
>
> — Harry S. Truman

MADE IN AMERICA

WALT DISNEY WAS APOLITICAL. DESPITE numerous attempts to recruit him to run for public office, Walt always refused. In a conversation with Ray Bradbury regarding the state of their home city, Los Angeles, Bradbury begged Walt to run for mayor. Walt replied, "Why be mayor when I am already King of Disneyland?"

To lead, Walt never needed politics, position, or power. He saw what needed to be done, so he did it. No one told him to add sound to cartoons, but that is what he did with Mickey Mouse in *Steamboat Willie*.

No one told him to take animation and create a full-length feature film, but that's what he did with *Snow White and the Seven Dwarfs*. No one told him to create a theme park—a place where parents and children could have fun together—but that's what he did with Disneyland. Lastly, no one told him to get into urban planning and work to solve the problems of the inner city, but that's exactly what he set out to do with EPCOT.

Walt may have been apolitical, but he was also unapologetically, passionately patriotic. To his core, Walt Disney was a turn-of-the-century Midwestern boy from Illinois who chased his dreams to California. Along the way, he never forgot who he was or where he was from. Abraham Lincoln was Walt's childhood hero, and Walt often dressed up like Lincoln and would recite, from memory, the *Gettysburg Address*. It is no surprise then that Walt assembled Honest Abe as the world's first human Audio-Animatronics figure to star at the 1964-65 World's Fair for the Illinois Pavilion. When the exhibit opened inside Disneyland's Main Street Opera House in 1965, Lincoln Savings and Loan sponsored the show—a show where guests often observed Walt exiting the theater in tears. Further, Walt offered the show for free to guests seventeen years of age or younger "so that young people may become better acquainted with one of the greatest figures in American History."

> *"Actually, if you could see close in my eyes,*
> *the American flag is waving in both of them and*
> *up my spine is glowing this red, white, and blue stripe."*
>
> — Walt Disney

WHAT DOES IT MEAN TO BE AN AMERICAN?

WHEN I TEACH AMERICAN HISTORY, I always start with this question, "What does it mean to be an American?" In today's politically charged times, this is a difficult question, but it has *always* been a difficult question. Yes, Americans have come from different locations, but we have also landed in different locations. Life in colonial New England looked nothing like life in the antebellum Deep South. Four hundred years later, people living on the East Coast have a very different "American" experience than those living on the West Coast.

As I was making this point one semester in Arizona, an Army First Sergeant sitting in the first row raised his hand and agreed with me 100 percent. "You are so right, Dr. Barnes. There is no single definition of what it means to be an American. For that matter, my wife and I both grew up in Florida, and the two of us cannot even agree on what it means to be a Floridian."

Given that I, too, am from Florida, my ears piqued up as he continued, "You see, I am from Jacksonville. Jacksonville is a *real* city. Why, we even have a National Football League team, the Jacksonville Jaguars." Given their deplorable record, I was tempted to debate the legitimacy of calling the Jaguars an "NFL team," but, for once, I held my tongue.

"My wife, however, comes from the panhandle. The panhandle is *very* different from the rest of Florida." Being that I, too, hail from the panhandle, *now* the First Sergeant really had me listening. "Compared to the metropolis that is Jacksonville, my wife comes from the most pedestrian, parochial, and Podunk town you can possibly imagine. You wouldn't believe how backwards those people are, Dr. Barnes. And yet, she is always saying we are both 'from Florida.'"

Curious, I inquired further, "First Sergeant, what is the name of the small town your wife is from?"

"Oh, you and the rest of the class wouldn't have ever heard of it, Dr. Barnes. Not all the way out here in Arizona," he responded.

"Try me," I urged.

"Well, she comes from this place just outside of Fort Walton Beach. A little town called Niceville."

"First Sergeant, before you say another word, I think it best that I share with you, and the rest of our class, that I am a graduate of Niceville Senior High School in Niceville, Florida."

The First Sergeant sat in stunned silence. The rest of the class could not believe the coincidence. *What are the odds?* they wondered. The next day, I brought in my Niceville Senior High School diploma from May 1981—what we historians like to call a "primary source document."

Knowing what it means to be a leader is about as easy as knowing what it means to be an American. Everyone has a different definition. What I do know is that being an American has never been about where you are from. America is about where you are going. The same is true for leadership. When leading, people don't care about where you've been—past credentials, past experiences, past exploits. What they care about is *their* future—and as much as Walt Disney was patriotic about the past, he was equally fervent about moving forward into the future. A future that included an Experimental Prototype Community of Tomorrow where, according to Walt, "the people will be king."

THE AMERICAN ADVENTURE

WHEN IT FIRST OPENED, EPCOT was the future. "The 21st Century Begins October 1, 1982," was more than an opening day marketing slogan. It was a vision. This vision for tomorrow was first found in the front section of Epcot, Future World. Yet, oddly enough, the most futuristic attraction found in Epcot on opening day was in the rear of World Showcase by way of its centerpiece attraction, the American Adventure.

Initially, Imagineers planned to place the American Adventure at the entrance of World Showcase, but then they realized it would be too close to Future World, and worse, block the stunning views of the reflecting lagoon. Instead, they placed the ginormous but stately Georgian colonial-style structure in the center of the other pavilions so it could act as "host" for the other countries. Like America, its size serves to draw people in. It *is* the castle of World Showcase, and it beckons people to the back portion of the park.

Unlike Great Moments with Mr. Lincoln at Disneyland or the Hall of Presidents at the Magic Kingdom, the American Adventure is hosted by iconic Americans who, like Walt Disney, never needed a political position as a platform for leadership. According to Jeff Kurti, Benjamin Franklin was picked "for his cheery gifts of insight and invention," while Mark Twain was tapped "for his circumspect outlook and wry humor."

Franklin and Twain come to life as Audio-Animatronics figures; at the time, they were the most sophisticated Disney had ever designed. The "play," the first ever put on by a Disney park, begins with the landing of the *Mayflower*, and like the pilgrims and their own American adventure, the show had a rough start. The complex Audio-Animatronics figures rarely functioned properly. Unlike the opening of Magic Kingdom, where attractions matched and mirrored the time-tested rides and shows from Disneyland, everything in Epcot was brand new. In his history of Walt Disney World, *Realityland*, David Koenig writes regarding Epcot that "there weren't any duplications; they were all prototypical. The shows' actions, especially for American Adventure, you didn't know if they were going to work until you put them together."

America remains the world's greatest experiment. Can it work? Is it working? Will it work? These were the questions in 1776, and we are still asking these questions today. The answers rest not in the government but in each individual's daily decisions. Your success is far more dependent on *you* than whoever may or may not be in Washington. Thus, the American Adventure closes with these words from Thomas Wolfe: "To all people, regardless of their birth, the right to live, to work, to be themselves, and to become whatever their visions can combine to make them. This is the promise of America."

"To be thrown upon one's own resources, is to be
cast into the very lap of fortune, for our faculties then

*undergo a development and display an energy of which
they were previously unsusceptible."*

— Benjamin Franklin
Audio-Animatronics Co-Host of
the American Adventure

LIBERTY STREET

DESPITE THE MASSIVE PROPORTIONS OF the American Adventure's
pavilion, this is not the largest space dedicated to the ideals of American
independence, and our dependence on individualism, inside a Disney
park. This honor goes to Liberty Square. Liberty Square is located
between Fantasyland and Frontierland at Florida's Magic Kingdom,
but the idea came from California and a design originally destined for
Disneyland. In 1956, only one year after opening day, Walt Disney
announced that the park's first expansion would be Liberty Street.

Located behind the east side of Main Street, plans for Liberty
Street included a Hall of Presidents. This Hall of Presidents predated
Audio-Animatronics so the various presidents would have been mere
mannequins. Before you mock the mannequins, remember that Andrew
Jackson is the first President ever to make a Disney park appearance.
A mannequin mockup of Old Hickory was present at Disneyland, on
opening day, in the Davy Crockett exhibit found in Frontierland. For
a variety of reasons, Liberty Street was never built at Disneyland but,
instead, debuted as Liberty Square, with its centerpiece attraction the
Hall of Presidents, on opening day at Walt Disney World in 1971.

Speaking of liberty and freedom, you know you are leading yourself
when you show up in Florida and ask the state to grant you permission
to form your own government. This is exactly what Disney did in 1967
when it worked with the Florida legislature and governor to create
the Reedy Creek Improvement District and two municipalities, Bay

Lake and Lake Buena Vista. The two municipalities limit voting rights to property owners, of which there are only forty-seven—all Disney employees. Except for the payment of property taxes and the issuing of elevator permits, Disney is its own government at Walt Disney World. According to Stephanie Barczewski, "Disney's power over its property was so great that Governor Claude Kirk joked to Roy when he signed the legislation that "[I]t's very comprehensive. I noticed only one omission. You made no provision for the crown."

BE CAREFUL WHAT YOU ASK FOR

PARENTING IS A FORM OF government. Personally, in a family situation, I prefer dictatorship over democracy, but like countries, every family has the right to form its own sovereign state of dysfunction. Our boys learned early how to do their own laundry, a weekly chore that exacerbates Wesley. Affectionately called "Messley," he has yet to see the point of washing, drying, and folding clothes with the regularity we require.

One weekend, Wesley was doing his clothes "the Wesley way," which meant throwing everything from one laundry basket into the washer, then into the dryer, and then back into the laundry basket. Taking cues from my mother, I insisted that each article of clothing be folded or hung properly. Frustrated, he screamed louder than any rebel in Colonial America, "I can't wait until I am out on my own. I can't wait until I am old enough to have my own place! Where I can be independent! I can't wait until I can do what *I* want to do the way *I* want to do it!"

I jumped up and raced toward him. I surprised him when, rather than a rebuke, I offered him an energetic high-five. "Congratulations, Wes! We finally agree on something! Both of us want the *exact same thing!*"

Wes was less than amused. We all want freedom. We forget, however, that with freedom comes responsibility. It is much easier to rely on others; our parents, our spouse, our boss, our political leaders, and then make them responsible for what isn't working in our lives. Real leaders do their own laundry. We don't wait for Washington to take out the wash. And when things go badly, and they inevitably will, we don't blame others and then hang them out to dry for our own mistakes.

SOUVENIR STOP

POOH FOR PRESIDENT—IN 1972, AND again in 1976, Disney supported a Winnie the Pooh for President campaign. Sponsored by Sears, Eeyore served as campaign manager and Tigger took his turn as Press Secretary. "Pooh in '72" promised "honey in every pot" and campaigned across the country with a whistle-stop tour that started with a ticker-tape parade down Main Street, U.S.A. Rivals readily admitted that the bear "made more sense than any other candidate."

Before you "pooh pooh" the idea of Pooh for President, reflect first on Pooh's primary platform: "You're braver than you believe, stronger than you seem, and smarter than you think." As you think about leading yourself, remember a time when you were in fact:

Braver than you believed.

Stronger than you seemed.

Smarter than you thought.

I'M NOT A CROOK—POOH LOST the 1972 election to the reelection efforts of Republican Richard M. Nixon. During that summer, while Pooh was parading at Disneyland, Nixon was busy bugging Washington's Watergate Hotel, the headquarters for the Democratic National Convention. The ensuing cover-up resulted in Nixon's resignation in 1974. In between, Nixon made a trip to Walt Disney World in 1973. His press secretary, Ron Ziegler, a former Jungle Cruise skipper at Disneyland, arranged for Nixon to make remarks at the Associated Press Convention held at the Contemporary Resort. On November 17, 1973, Nixon stood in front of four hundred reporters and three national networks who were carrying the event live. Frustrated by the wave of Watergate questions, Nixon stared directly into the cameras and said, "The people have to know whether or not their president is a crook. Well, I'm not a crook!"

"I'm not a crook" became an instant catchphrase, and it came to us live from Walt Disney World! I am going to trust that you are, in fact, not a crook. But leaders need to know who they are rather than focusing on who they are not. What do you believe are your greatest strengths, and how can these strengths help your success and enable you to lead yourself as well as others?

CHOOSE THE SINGLE RIDER LINE—MANY Disney attractions give guests the option of waiting in a single rider line. Yes, you will experience the attraction separately from your friends and family, but your wait time is significantly shorter. The same is true for your dreams and goals. Stop waiting for everyone to give you permission to start living your life. Don't wait to find a publisher to write your book, a boss to start your business, or a companion to travel the world. Lead yourself by choosing yourself!

> *"Be who you are, not who anyone else is,*
> *or who anyone else wants you to be."*
>
> — James Altucher

GETTING YOUR HAND STAMPED

WHEN WALT OPENED DISNEYLAND ON July 17, 1955, he recruited his friend, Art Linkletter, to serve as Master of Ceremonies for the live ABC broadcast. Viewed by 90 million Americans that Sunday, the broadcast also featured co-hosts Bob Cummings and another friend of Walt's, Ronald Reagan.

In my History of Disneyland class, we take time to view, via YouTube, the entire show. Students are shocked by several scenes, scenes they see as ancient history etched in black and white. Without fail, there is always an audible gasp when Reagan first appears on screen. "Wow, how was Walt able to get the President of the United States to help him open Disneyland?" they ask. "That's incredible!"

The answer, of course, is that in 1955 Ronald Reagan wasn't yet President. In fact, in 1955, he was a B-grade Hollywood actor and still several years away from his political career. On July 17, 1955, Ronald Reagan could no more envision leading himself to the White House than Walt Disney could imagine Disneyland being such a success that he would one day want to expand on it by embarking on the creation of an Experimental Prototype Community of Tomorrow. When Epcot opened on October 1, 1982, Walt's friend, Ronald Reagan, occupied the White House and sent these words of congratulations to the world:

> Nancy and I are delighted to extend our warmest congratulations and best wishes to everyone gathered for the Grand Opening of Disney World's Epcot Center.
>
> This historical moment marks the realization of a singular vision of the future by a great man and an outstanding organization. Epcot Center stands as a tribute to the technical know-how of American industry and the inventiveness of the human mind. There is far more here than the thrills and delights of amusement, for Epcot is truly a doorway to the twenty-first century and destined to become an integral part of the American experience. In presenting solutions to problems faced by communities and nations around the globe, it will be a showcase for the free enterprise system and optimism of the American spirit.

Walt Disney's achievements brought happiness to the hearts of young and old alike. He once referred to his own work as

"Imagineering," and he was quick to utilize the talents and creativity of others to take us to a place no one else had ever been, where we would leave the comfort of the familiar and enter the world of the pioneer, and where imagination and dedication combined to make dreams a reality.

Epcot Center is the product of a man who dared to dream and had the courage and drive to accomplish that dream. When asked for the secret of his success, Walt replied, "I simply wished upon a star." That star will now illuminate the lives of youngsters, Americans, and people from around the world who enter here and experience the ingenuity, history, showmanship, and hope of Epcot Center.

We join all Americans in wishing you great success as you point the way to the future.

Reagan's election hinged on the hope of less government and more individual freedom. In other words, learn to lead yourself. Americans took Reagan's message to heart, and in 1984, they reelected him in a landslide. Ironically enough, the president credited with winning the Cold War missed much of his second inauguration on January 21, 1985 due to the dangerously cold conditions in Washington, DC. The temperature that day was -4°F with a windchill factor of -20°F. Officials moved a few of the festivities indoors, but almost everything else was cancelled, including the traditional inaugural parade.

More bitter than the cold was the disappointment of some twenty-five high school marching bands that had been invited to perform. Disney took the lead by offering "the sunny climes of Walt Disney World as a replacement for the parade." So, on Monday May 27, 1985— Memorial Day—President Reagan landed via helicopter behind the American Adventure pavilion in Epcot and enjoyed the only inaugural parade ever to take place outside of the nation's capital.

On that special day, the American president didn't even make the most notable appearance. That honor was reserved for Mickey Mouse. Remember how Disney excluded him from Epcot when the park opened in 1982? New leadership arrived in 1984. With new leadership came new decisions. Michael Eisner and Frank Wells took charge and used the president's inauguration as the perfect opportunity for the official welcome of Mickey into Epcot for the first time.

He and his friends have been leading guests there ever since.

*"There are no constraints on the human mind,
no walls around the human spirit, no barriers to
our progress except those we erect ourselves."*

— Ronald Reagan

FINDING THE TIME

"The evolution of a theme park doesn't really follow a time clock, calendar, or any other arbitrary man-made measure."

— Jack Lindquist
Former Disneyland President and Disney Legend

"THE 21ST CENTURY BEGINS"

EPCOT WAS ALWAYS A BOLD vision. Whether it was Walt dreaming of a domed, progress city where individuals and corporations could live together, work together, and dream together, *or* the hybrid world's fair/futuristic theme park that Disney ultimately opened in October 1982, Epcot has always been both eclectic and eccentric.

What *is* Epcot?

I can remember asking that question when passing the park and an unfinished Spaceship Earth on my way to the Magic Kingdom for my Grad Night celebration in May 1981. The world was still seventeen months away from finally getting to experience the realized version of Walt's Experimental Prototype Community of Tomorrow, but the Disney marketing machine was already in full force. Everywhere I looked, posters were promoting the opening of Epcot and proclaiming that "The 21st Century Begins October 1, 1982."

Today, I'm not sure what is more startling. Disney's declaration that it could jump-start a new millennia eighteen years early, the fact that we are now seventeen years deep into the twenty-first century, or that it has been more than thirty-six years since I graduated from high school. Where has the time gone?

I have no idea!

But here is what I do know: Dreams and success take both time and money. You can always make more money, but time is your only non-renewable resource. And your clock is *always* ticking.

> *"Time is life's most valuable commodity*
> *and attracts many robbers."*
>
> — Author Unknown

TICK-TOCK

WALT DISNEY TAUGHT ME HOW to tell time. Well, technically, it was Walt's alter-ego, Mickey Mouse, who taught me how to tell time. I received a Mickey Mouse watch for graduation—my graduation from kindergarten in 1969—and I used it endlessly during elementary school as teachers taught me how to read a clock, take timed tests, and measure my day. Decades later, I still wear a Mickey Mouse watch—a gift from Niki in honor of my first paid, professional presentation on *The Wisdom of Walt: Leadership Lessons from the Happiest Place on Earth*.

And I am not alone.

Generations of children grew up wearing Mickey Mouse watches. Mickey's rise in popularity was serendipitously timed with the depths of the Great Depression. Walt introduced Mickey just months before the 1929 stock market crash. It wasn't just the synchronized sound in *Steamboat Willie* that resonated with the American people. It was also Mickey's indomitable spirit—a spirit that was in short supply as world economic reports grew bleaker and bleaker.

Statistically, the Great Depression lasted until the United States officially entered World World II in December 1941. It reached its peak, however, in 1933 when unemployment stood at a staggering 33 percent and our Gross Domestic Product was zero. Take heart, however, because 1933 is also the year Disney introduced its first Mickey Mouse timepiece. Over the next two years, cash-strapped Americans purchased more than two million Mickey Mouse watches.

Our world has certainly changed since 1933. Today, most Americans feel way more over-employed than under-employed or even unemployed. In our current culture, being "busy" and "not having enough time" is a badge of honor.

Think about it.

When was the last time you asked someone how he was doing and he responded with, "You know, I don't have nearly enough to do," or "I have more time on my hands than I know what to do with, but thanks for asking." It is un-American, if not inhuman, not to be busy!

But are you *really* that busy?

With a full-time job as a higher education administrator, as a faculty member who teaches every semester, as an author/speaker, and as a husband/father, I am asked from time to time, "With everything you have going on, when do you find time to write?"

I have several responses to this question. But my favorite answer is, "In between my naps."

On the surface, this comes off as both smug and sarcastic. But I won't apologize for making the time to see my dreams come true.

And neither should you.

People do what they want to do. So ask yourself this question: Do you really not have enough time, or are you like the crocodile, Tick-Tock, in Peter Pan, except instead of swallowing an alarm clock, you've swallowed the line of "busyness" that everyone else is spouting to mask your fears?

Oh, snap!

*"Being busy is a form of laziness—lazy thinking
and indiscriminate action."*

— Tim Ferriss

WHAT TIME IS THE THREE O'CLOCK PARADE?

WALT DISNEY ONCE SAID, "[I]n Disneyland, clocks and watches
will lose all meaning for there is no present. There is only yesterday,
tomorrow, and the timeless land of fantasy." He believed this so strongly
that he reinforced the idea by having these words written over the
Magic Kingdom entrance tunnels, ""Here you leave today and enter
the world of yesterday, tomorrow and fantasy."

And yet, Disney parks everywhere are filled with clocks. The first is
found at the front of each Magic Kingdom via the Main Street railroad
station. The stations in California and Florida are different and distinct,
but both feature timepieces at the tops of their towers. This is fitting
because before the arrival of the railroad, every local town kept its
own time according to "high noon." It was the railroad and the need
to coordinate transcontinental schedules that forced us to get serious
about time and develop standardized time zones.

One of the more interesting stories from the early days of Disneyland
is how the Main Street Train Station clock did *not* keep a standardized
time. Jim Korkis explains further in *Secret Stories of Disneyland*:

> When Disneyland opened in 1955, for the first few
> months, one of the most frequent complaints from the
> guests was that the clock on the Main Street Train Station
> showed the incorrect time. They were trying to use it to
> coordinate their day, and it was always wrong. Each day, the
> Maintenance Department was sent to correct the problem,
> but the complaints continued.

Again, and again, a diligent maintenance staff member went to the station, set up a ladder and carefully reset the clock. Later that day, the complaints continued.

Was there something wrong with the gears? Was the California heat affecting the mechanisms? Was there foul play from a disgruntled employee?

Management set out to investigate and questioned the person who would re-set the clock.

"I try to be as accurate as possible," stated the man. "I call the operator at the Park to get the correct time, set my own watch and then climb the tower to set the station clock."

Further investigation continued of the incorrect time on the clock. Finally, it was decided to check every step of the procedure. A man was stationed next to the operator in the Main Street City Hall. When she received the call from Maintenance for the correct time, she looked out her window and told him the time she saw on the train station clock.

I believe Disneyland is timeless. I also believe it is a reminder of the importance of time. Dreams and success need a schedule. Look out your window, think about your dreams, and set your watch accordingly. Everyone and everything else will adjust.

Disney's unstated goal is that an average guest, on an average operating day, will be able to experience, on average, ten Magic Kingdom attractions. Take a tour of Disneyland with Niki and me and we can nearly double that—by 3 p.m. Here is the itinerary: Peter Pan, Alice, Tea Cups, Dumbo, Casey Junior, Carrousel, Mr. Toad, Pinocchio, Snow White, Jungle Cruise, Pirates of the Caribbean, Space Mountain, Star

Tours, Walt Disney's Enchanted Tiki Room, Indiana Jones, Matterhorn, Haunted Mansion, Splash Mountain, and Big Thunder Mountain. This leaves you with plenty of time for parades, fireworks, shows, shopping, restaurants, and other favorite attractions. How will you spend your newfound afternoon and evening?

The primary reason we can accomplish so much in so little time is because we *have a plan.* We know exactly what time we are arriving at the park (thirty minutes before opening), we know exactly where to line up (turnstile 13), we know exactly where we are going first (Peter Pan and Fantasyland), and we know exactly who is getting Fastpasses (Niki) and in what order (Space, Star Tours, Indy, Matterhorn, Splash, Big Thunder), and we have alternate plans that adjust when the park opens later, an attraction is under refurbishment, or a ride is suddenly shuttered.

How do you plan your work day? Do you know what you are trying to accomplish—when, where, and why? Or do you just show up and immediately go into react and respond mode?

> *"You'll never have enough money to buy all the stuff you don't really need, and you'll never have enough time to do all the things you really don't want to do."*
>
> — Gay Hendricks

YOU'RE LATE! YOUR'E LATE!

THE SUMMER BEFORE HIS FRESHMAN year in high school, our oldest son, Logan, started playing football. This was a bit of a stretch for all of us. Me, because I don't have an athletic bone in my body. Niki, like any mom, was concerned about concussions and her son's safety. Logan, because he is far more electronically inclined than he is any kind of sports enthusiast. Nonetheless, we supported Logan's decision because it represented an opportunity for him to be on a team and to go outside his comfort zone—something Niki and I support whenever possible.

The first challenge came not from Logan's first practice or first game. No, the first challenge came the first time we were "late" picking him up. Whenever we dropped him off for practice, we asked him when practice was over so we would know when to pick him up. Sometimes, practice would end sooner than anticipated or we might be delayed due to work, errands, or transporting his younger brother, Wesley, to his activities.

When I was a kid this happened *all the time*. My dad worked two jobs and my mom took care of four kids. There were times when I had to wait.

And wait.

And wait.

Today, lads like Logan are armed with a weapon we could only dream of in the 1970s. A communication device not featured in Disneyland's Tomorrowland of 1955 or the Magic Kingdom's Tomorrowland of 1971. A cellphone!

The second Logan stepped out of practice and neither Niki or I were there to transport him home, he would begin calling and texting.

"You're late, where are you?"

"Do you know where Mom is?"

"Hey, did Dad forget to pick me up?"

After enduring this one too many times, I sat Logan down and explained to him that he was overreacting. I broke into one of those dreaded *back-in-my-day* stories that every child loathes. "Logan, believe it or not, I played a few sports (albeit poorly) when I was a kid. My dad was always working and my mom was busy taking care of me, plus three more. I can't remember the number of times my parents were late and I had to wait after a practice. Sometimes the wait was a few minutes, sometimes the wait was an hour or more. I didn't have a cellphone and nobody died just because I had to wait."

We then agreed on a fifteen-minute window of waiting. If, after waiting fifteen minutes, his ride home had not appeared, *then* he could deploy his cellphone and start making cries for help. Logan learned quickly and honored our fifteen-minute window request from that day forward.

And then the student became the master.

A week before the start of Logan's second season of football, we traveled to San Francisco for the wedding of a close family friend. The morning after the wedding, our car wouldn't start. I called roadside assistance, and it promised help would arrive at our hotel at 9:45 a.m. Anxious to get on the road and start the eight-hour drive home, I was obviously annoyed when 9:45 a.m. arrived but roadside assistance was still nowhere to be found. By 9:55 a.m., I declared to Niki that the mechanic was already ten minutes late, so I was calling to find out what was taking so long.

Logan interjected immediately.

"Nope! It's only been ten minutes. He isn't late. We all know that everyone gets a fifteen-minute window before you can start texting, calling, and complaining. Put the phone down, Dad!"

Don't you hate it when that happens? You spend your life as a parent trying to teach your kids important life lessons, and then they manage to flip the lesson back on you.

I know you are in a hurry. I know we live in a world of seemingly instant gratification, and this goals/dreams/success stuff seems like it will take *f o r e v e r*.

Maybe even longer.

The amount of time it takes to accomplish anything of significance can discourage you from ever getting started. Why bother trying to find time out of your already busy schedule if it will take an eternity and you don't even have an hour today?

Stop trying to *find* time and start *making* time. Don't think about how much time it will all take. Instead, think about how much time you can make today. No one has an eternity today, but surely you can make a window—be it five or fifteen minutes that, over time, can start adding up. Fifteen minutes a day is close to one hundred hours a year.

What might your dream look like 365 days from now with one hundred hours of work behind it?

"Most people overestimate what they can do in
a year and they underestimate what they can do in
two or three decades."

— Tony Robbins

GETTING YOUR HAND STAMPED

WHOA! WHERE IS OUR SOUVENIR Stop for Finding the Time?

Most people don't realize that closing time at the Magic Kingdom is different from *exit* time. If the park closes at 11 p.m., that means you can be in line for an attraction, regardless of the wait time, and still experience the ride. In addition, Main Street traditionally stays open a full hour after the park "closes," so it won't be until midnight that cast members start ushering guests out of the park. To honor this tradition, I have strategically placed the Souvenir Stop at the end of the chapter—a reminder that you shouldn't waste valuable touring time when you have an extra hour at the end of the day to shop for souvenirs.

From groundbreaking in 1954 to opening day in 1955, it took exactly one year to build Disneyland. In contrast, groundbreaking in Florida took place in 1967 and Magic Kingdom didn't open until 1971. From day one, Florida has enjoyed the blessings of more money, more land, and more time than Walt could dream possible in the 1950s. Nonetheless, finishing Magic Kingdom following four years of construction was just as hectic as finishing Disneyland after only 365 days of building.

That's the way it goes with dreams and deadlines. You will never find the time unless you become intentional about making the time. Even then, you will be forced to squeeze minutes out of seconds as your project comes close to completion and you get so close to your goal that you can finally see the finish line—a finish line that is a mere mirage as you realize how much more you still must do. Along the way, remember what Walt once said, "Everyone needs deadlines."

One of the unfinished tasks when Magic Kingdom opened was a time capsule. Imagineers prepared a spot behind the bricks of Cinderella Castle for the capsule, but they simply ran out of time so the capsule was never completed. The unfinished time capsule became the stuff of urban legend and symbolic of the frantic finish. According to a story conveyed by Jim Korkis in *Secret Stories of Walt Disney World*, Ron Heminger, who began his career at Disneyland in 1955 and eventually became a manager at Epcot, got into a heated argument with his supervisor one day about whether there ever had been a time capsule.

> His supervisor, who was not there in those months of construction, laughed and told him it was just an urban legend and that there were never any plans for a time capsule. Heminger knew better and insisted that it was true and that a place had been prepared in Cinderella Castle.

> The discussion started to escalate, and Heminger finally told the supervisor to meet him at Cinderella Castle a few hours past park closing after the guests and maintenance staff had left.

> When the park closed, Heminger and one of his cohorts went to the Pirates of the Caribbean attraction and took a full skeleton. Then they went to Cinderella Castle and carefully removed a plaque. In the hollowed-out hole behind the plaque, a space had indeed been prepared for *something*.

> They dressed the skeleton in a distinctive WED (Walt Disney Imagineering) hard hat and vest, stuffed it into the opening, and then replaced the plaque.

Later that evening, Heminger met his supervisor at the agreed location and gave him a flashlight. With some theatrical difficulty, Heminger removed the plaque while he told how things were so hectic in the final days of building the Magic Kingdom that they basically spent their energy during the last few days just making sure everything was covered up for the guests until they could get to it again. The same thing had happened just before the opening of Disneyland and some things were never found later.

The supervisor was surprised to see a wide hole hidden behind the plaque. Turning on the flashlight, he curiously stuck his head deep inside and peered below...where he saw the supposed remains of a hapless WED employee inadvertently trapped and forgotten for years.

Please don't let your ideas, your goals, or your dreams become trapped and forgotten.

Capture the time necessary for living your life at the next level. The minutes, months, and years are going to pass regardless, so why not make the most of them?

> "Ten years from now we will surely arrive.
> The question is where?"
>
> — Tony Robbins

SOUVENIR STOP

I HOPE YOU ENJOYED YOUR full day at the park and experienced every possible attraction. Now that you know Main Street is open a full hour after the park closes, let's get some shopping done—a few keepsakes that will help us keep more of our most valuable resource, time.

PICK A HEADLINER—HEADLINE ATTRACTIONS ARE the must see, can't miss, do them no matter what experiences. Headline attractions vary from park to park and person to person, but they represent the number one priority for any touring plan.

Start your day by determining what your headline activity will be. Gary Keller, author of *The One Thing: The Surprisingly Simple Truth Behind Extraordinary Results*, advocates constantly asking yourself this question: "What's the ONE Thing you can do this day that by doing it everything else would be easier or unnecessary." Whatever that thing is, that becomes your priority and what you do first.

EASILY MISSED—I LOVE DISNEYLAND AND Walt Disney World. That doesn't mean, however, that I love every attraction. Some are worth my time, regardless of the line, and others are not, regardless of how short the wait might be.

The same truths apply to your daily activities. Stop answering every call the second your phone rings. Stop responding to every email the second your inbox "pings." Stop attending every mindless meeting just because you were invited. Batch as many tasks together as possible; for example, answer email once a day, return phone messages once a day, pay bills once a month, and minimize meetings.

Create your "Not to Do" List Below:

1. _____
2. _____
3. _____
4. _____

YOUR APPROXIMATE WAIT—WHEN WE TOOK Bethany to Disneyland at age five, she couldn't yet tell time and didn't understand the difference between a twenty-minute line and an hour-long wait. She loved watching Scooby Doo cartoons (the Mystery Machine makes it no mystery why today she is an investigative journalist), so we measured everything in twenty-minute increments; for example, this line is three Scooby Doos long.

You can do the same. When working on your headliner, Your One Big Thing, set a twenty-minute timer, block out all distractions, and *focus.* Think it doesn't work? I wrote *The Wisdom of Walt,* and am writing this book, in increments of Scooby Doo time—twenty-minute blocks of time.

"You can do so much in 10 minutes' time.
Ten minutes, once gone, are gone for good.
Divide your life into 10-minute units and sacrifice as few
of them as possible in meaningless anxiety."

— Ingvar Kamprad

WAKE UP, JOSE—NIKI AND I are big believers in the power of the Power Nap. So much so that I dream of writing a coffee-table book illustrating the best places to nap at Disneyland. My favorite sleep spot is inside the Tiki Room. I find a bench in the back, and when the cast member starts the show with "Wake Up, Jose," then it is "Goodnight, Jeff!" I awake with the thunderclap during the rainstorm, fresh as a flower, and ready to continue with my day.

Don't be embarrassed to nap. My daily naps are non-negotiable, and I've never angered the gods for doing so. Noted nappers include Thomas Edison, Winston Churchill, Gene Autry, and Ronald Reagan. Thanks to recent studies, we now know that nappers are more alert, healthy, and productive!

"Do what you should do now, so later you
can do what you want to do."

— Lee Cockerell

HAVING TO HUSTLE

"Good things may come to those who wait,
but only the things left by those who hustle."

— attributed to Abraham Lincoln
America's Sixteenth President and the World's First
Human Audio-Animatronics Figure

SOARIN' OVER SUCCESS

FROM THE BEGINNING, I HAD issues with the extremely popular attraction Soarin' Over California at Disney's California Adventure park. The ride itself was fine. In fact, it is one of mine and Niki's all-time favorites, and it was the only attraction enjoyed by everyone when the much-maligned park opened across from Disneyland in February 2001.

The attraction was such a hit that it is one of the few attractions from Disneyland's "second gate" to be exported anywhere else, finding its home in Walt Disney World's "second gate," Epcot, in 2005 and at Shanghai Disneyland in 2016. The attraction was always popular in California and even more so in Epcot. This was true even before Disney switched the flying simulator to the new *Soarin' Around the World* film (developed for Shanghai)—a theme much better suited for Epcot.

Credit for the ingenious design of the ride experience of this combination IMAX movie theatre and hang-gliding simulator belongs to Mark Sumner. Struggling to come up with a concept that would work and not be cost-prohibitive, one night Mark remembered an old Erector Set from his childhood that was still sitting in his garage. He rumbled through the remains and strung together enough pieces to erect a working model that showed it was possible to load eighty-seven guests per theatre, on a single level, and then lift them forward into the concavity of the screen. This creates the sensation of flight and restricts the view of the riders to the images projected onto the screen.

Again, a *great* attraction!

My issue isn't with the ride or even the queue. My issue is with the pre-show safety spiel hosted by Patrick Warburton. Patrick voiced the character Kronk in the 2000 Disney movie *The Emperor's New Groove,* but he is no doubt best-remembered for his role as Puddy on the smash television comedy *Seinfeld*—fitting for this situation because I am about to do some major mocking. Here is Puddy's—I mean Patrick's—narration:

> Hello, and welcome to Soarin'. My name is Patrick, and I'll be your chief flight attendant today. We'll begin boarding in a few minutes, but first, I'd like to acquaint you with some important safety information.
>
> When the doors to your flight open, please take a seat and store all carry-on items in the under-seat compartment. This includes cameras, purses, hats, and of course, these little beauties [Mickey Mouse ears]. Next, fasten your seatbelt, inserting them into the buckle on your right. If smaller aviators don't measure up to the height indicator on the seat, just put the belt through the loop in the center strap before buckling.
>
> *Nice work, pal!* [Here Patrick gives a thumbs up.]

Soon you will be airborne, so if you or your little aviators have a fear of flying or of heights, you might want to wait for your party at the arrival gate. Okay, let's review: that is seat, seatbelt, carry-on items, safety strap, fear of heights, keep your hands and arms inside at all times—anything else?

Oh, yeah, have a nice flight!

Nice work, pal?

Go back to the ride and watch the video. You will see that the "smaller aviator," an older child, never moves a muscle as his belt is passed through the loop and buckled for him by his mother. Yet, he gets a big thumbs up and a "Nice work, pal" from Patrick.

For what?

He didn't do anything!

For more than fifteen years, while waiting to board Soarin' Over California, I watched this video repeatedly. Like an Audio-Animatronics figure triggered by a passing sensor, I voiced my complaint each and every time:

"He didn't do anything!"

With the introduction of Soarin' Around the World in 2016, I was looking forward to a new pre-show spiel and the elimination of Patrick's thumbs up and "Nice work, pal" for the kid who never moved a muscle.

Nope!

The attraction may have changed, but the pre-show spiel remains as static as the boy who never moves a muscle—dooming another generation of smaller aviators into believing they deserve a thumbs up and "Nice work, pal" for doing *absolutely nothing*!

DIGGING DITCHES

I DON'T CARE WHO YOU are.

I don't care where you live.

I don't care what your goal or dream may be.

What I do care about is your success. Yes, I want to see everyone's dreams come true. So I need to speak a word of truth here that might not be welcome in today's world.

Success is *hard* work.

Dreams are really, *really hard* work.

At some point, you are going to have to roll up your sleeves, get to work, move your muscles, and hustle! Regardless of your idea, dream, or vision, none of it will ever matter unless you are willing to put in extraordinary effort to make things happen. The world doesn't give anyone a thumbs up or a "Nice work, pal" just for showing up.

The magic of the Magic Kingdom doesn't just happen, either. In his leadership book *Creating Magic*, Lee Cockerell, former Vice President of Operations for Walt Disney World, writes, "It's not the magic that makes it work; it's the way we *work* that makes it magic." Most of the operational hard work of the park takes place backstage, behind the scenes, or underground—unnoticed and under-appreciated by the guests who are there to escape the daily grind of their own jobs.

But having a job at Walt Disney World means having to work.

And just because we don't happen to see it doesn't mean someone isn't hustling.

For example, the primary task in creating Walt Disney World's first phase, which included opening the Magic Kingdom, involved the menial task of digging ditches. Lots of them. In the 1960s, there was a reason why 27,440 acres of land were undeveloped and available for purchase in Central Florida—it was "acre after acre of wet, boggy swampland." Disney and the State of Florida formed the Reedy Creek Drainage District in May 1966 authorizing the digging of ditches, drains, and canals that made development possible. Jeff Kurti provides this description in *Before the World Began*:

The first task for the Reedy Creek Drainage District was to develop methods to drain areas of swampland for construction without damaging the balance of the fragile water tables, and avoiding the ever-present danger of flooding. Since the whole of central Florida essentially floats on a body of freshwater, any depletion or damage to one part of this water supply could cause environmental imbalance and devastation to the entire region. After extensive planning, some 55 miles of canals and levees were constructed to control and exchange water levels without depleting the overall reserve. Water control schemes keep the water levels in check by automatically floating open when the water level peaks and then automatically closing when those peaks subside. The gates require no monitoring, and they remove the risk of flooding or drought. Instead of following the invasive straight lines of most artificial canal systems, the intricate network of canals on Disney property is designed to follow the curves of the natural landscape, an idea originally conceived by John Hench.

By design, guests shouldn't see or notice the first work ever done at Walt Disney World. The same will be true for you and your dream. If you want to make it happen then you will find yourself waking up and getting to work before everyone else and staying up and working well after everyone else has called it a day. Why? Because your dream demands nothing less. Jon Acuff writes about it this way:

You will work harder at something you love than at something you like. You will work harder than you have ever worked when you start chasing your dream. You will hustle and grind and sweat and push and pull. You will get up earlier and go to bed later. But that's okay. Know why? Joy is an incredible alarm clock. It will wake you up and keep you up and pick you up and gently pull you through a thousand rejections along the way. If your goal is to work less, stay on the road to average. Do something you just kind of like. Settle into life like a long winter's nap and coast on through to your 80s. But if you want to dream—if you want to live out some unique talent you've been given to steward during your time on this planet—get used to 4 a.m. alarms.

4 a.m.? Welcome to Magic Morning!

> *"Even though I have tremendously enjoyed what I have been doing for the past fifty years I have to point out that yet, it has been work. Sometimes hard, sometimes frustrating, always stimulating."*
>
> — Tony Baxter

CHEATERS NEVER PROSPER

HAVING TO HUSTLE CAN MEAN anything from working hard, working harder, to working smarter and faster. However, hustling does not mean cutting corners or hustling someone else for something that doesn't belong to you or something you didn't earn from your own efforts.

For example, I have had students fail my History of Disneyland class. They don't fail because they lack academic aptitude. They fail because they fail to put in any effort or, worse, they cheat. It is so sad to start the summer talking about our dreams and "The Happiest Place on Earth," only eight weeks later to have my students receive "Fs" on their transcripts because they failed to show up, failed to do the work, or failed because they plagiarized by passing off the hard work of others as their own.

One of the course's major assignments is to write a research paper on your favorite Disneyland attraction. I challenge students to explore the attraction's history, the story it is trying to tell, how the attraction has adapted and evolved over the years, and to compare/contrast the attraction with other versions at other Disney parks, if applicable. I recognize that students don't like writing research papers. But this is a college course, and if you can't get excited to write a paper about your favorite Disneyland attraction, then why take the class?

I've heard students defend their plagiarism, (for example, copying and pasting the readily recognizable words from the attraction's marketing description at Disneyland.com) with excuses like "Oh, the Internet must have stolen my paper," or "Yes, a *few* words *might* be copied and pasted, but I still worked my *ass* off on that paper!"

No, no you didn't.

Students who want an "A" just for showing up, or people who want a participation trophy just for signing up, remind me of a story from Walt himself, a story retold by Marty Sklar in *Dream It! Do It! My Half-Century Creating Disney's Magic Kingdoms*:

> A Disney Studio television producer was unhappy because Walt did not consider him to be "creative." Determined to change Walt's view, and recalling Walt's own handiwork on his backyard trains and miniatures built in the workshop barn at his Holmby Hills home, the producer spent weeks making a model to show Walt. He arrived early one morning and set up his work in Walt's outer office, insisting that Walt view his efforts before starting his day. Enthused over the product of weeks of work, the producer waited for Walt's reaction; however, none was forthcoming. "Well," the producer lamented, "at least you can give me 'E for Effort'". Reacting at last, Walt replied: "I'll give you "S for Shit.'"

"We dream of instant success, devoid of effort or struggle or denial. And, who could argue with the desire for a little

more ease along the way. But the truth is, all too often,
success without effort is hollow."

— Jonathan Fields

A DOOR IS OPENING…THIS TIME IT'S OPENING FOR YOU!

WALT DISNEY'S WORLD'S THIRD THEME park, the Disney-MGM Studios Theme Park (called Disney's Hollywood Studios today), opened on May 1, 1989. The idea for a studio-based theme park goes all the way back to Burbank and the days before Disneyland when Walt wanted to build Mickey Mouse Park on eight acres of available land adjacent to the Disney Studio. In the 1980s, Imagineers were working on plans for an Epcot expansion that included an Entertainment Pavilion where they could tell show business stories from Broadway, television, and Hollywood. When Disney's new leadership team, made up of Michael Eisner and Frank Wells, saw the plans, they took the expansion idea further and exploded it into a full-fledged park adjacent to Epcot. All of this coincided with Universal Studios' announcement that it planned to build an East Coast version of its Hollywood park and film studio experience on the 400 acres of land it had purchased between downtown Orlando and Walt Disney World.

While Universal waited for a financial partner, Disney beat them to the punch by partnering with MGM and hustling to open MGM-Hollywood Studios a full year before Universal Studios Florida was ready for its first visitors. According to Marty Sklar, "Suddenly, Michael and Frank were drenching us [with ideas]—and the Imagineers were cranking out drawings as fast as they could. As quick as you could say, 'Let's get there first!' we were off on a sprint to the finish." Expediting everything was made possible through the governmental control Disney enjoyed via its Reedy Creek Development deal with the State of Florida.

Aside from beating out a competitor, the goal for the Disney-MGM Studios park was to extend the time guests spent on Disney property without falling into the inevitable Epcot pitfalls—spending billions to get it built, spreading it out on too much land, and using innovative but unproven ride systems for new attractions. According to David Koenig in *Realityland*, "[T]he new plan was to add a 'half-day park,' more modest in scope and affordable to build than the other two [the Magic Kingdom and Epcot], but flashy enough to persuade the average vacationer to extend his or her stay by an extra day. They could spend the rest of their third-gate day at the Magic Kingdom or EPCOT."

During that first summer, sell-out crowds swelled Disney-MGM Studios. Guests quickly did the math, however, and realized they had paid full-price for what was clearly, at best, a half-day park. The new park opened with all of five attractions, only two of which were real rides—The Great Movie Ride and the Studio Backlot Tour. Even with extended operating hours, lines for everything surpassed sixty minutes or more barely an hour after park opening each day. Some guests felt "hustled," especially those who had purchased single-day tickets for the sole purpose of going to Disney-MGM Studios:

> "We got complaints," admitted Jim Moore, recalling guest reaction to pricing, congestion and limited attractions during the park's first months. "We had been told [to inform guests] that quality wasn't measured in size. But guests were paying the same price as Magic Kingdom and EPCOT for a park that was one-third the size. I remember giving full refunds."

Disney-MGM Studios started standing on its own when it opened my favorite Florida attraction, the Twilight Zone Tower of Terror, in July 1994. In creating this signature, E-ticket thrill ride, Imagineers watched every *Twilight Zone* episode, all 150 of them, twice. They even contracted Otis Elevator to help develop the ride system. But since Otis was in the business of making sure elevators *didn't* plummet down shafts, a specialized ride vendor was eventually brought on board to develop the faster-than-gravity drop experience. Exterior architecture includes echoes from the Mission Inn, a hotel just a few miles from my and Niki's home in Riverside, California, and inside, a near-perfect miniature replica of the tea room at the Millennium Biltmore in Los Angeles. At 199 feet, the Twilight Zone Tower of Terror is the second tallest structure at Walt Disney World (after Expedition Everest at 199.5 feet), and easily viewable from Epcot—thus, the exterior colors intentionally match the Morocco Pavilion in World Showcase.

Disney has since opened truncated versions of its Twilight Zone Tower of Terror: First in Anaheim, in 2004, to help the then-struggling Disney California Adventure Park, and again in 2008, in Paris, to help the underperforming Hollywood Studios Park adjacent to Disneyland Paris (a version without the *Twilight Zone* theme opened at Tokyo DisneySea in 2006). By my count, that is three times Disney has "dropped" the *Twilight Zone*-themed Tower of Terror into one of its parks to help "elevate" performance. I've ridden all three, but Florida's version remains my favorite because it is the only one where the elevator exits its shaft and moves guests forward through a dark, mirror-filled and starlit hallway. The elevator then enters another shaft where you randomly experience one of four computer-generated drop sequences. When I rode Tower of Terror in Florida for the first time in 2013, after having first experienced the lesser versions in California (2009) and Paris (2010), one word came to mind: *shafted!*

Disney recently converted California's Tower of Terror from a *Twilight Zone* theme to *Guardians of the Galaxy: Mission Breakout.* Some local fans are outraged by the change, but I am fine with it. Again, California's version has never been my favorite and, despite my disdain for the endless release of comic book/superhero movies, I like *Guardians of the Galaxy.*

Speaking of *Guardians of the Galaxy* and *Mission Breakout*, I want to share with you an Instagram post by Chris Pratt, the actor who plays the lead role of Peter Quill/Star-Lord in the Guardians of the Galaxy series. Here is what "breakout success" looks like:

January 30, 2016

It's 3:20 a.m. I got picked up for work at 6:45 a.m. yesterday. I'm not good with math, especially after being up for approximately 61 hours but I think I've been up for over 77 hours. I did a table read for Guardians of the Galaxy 2 this morning and then shot all day on Passengers and just now wrapped some 144 hours later. Weirdly both films, which I'll be shooting back to back, are being shot in Atlanta at Pinewood studios. We have the best crew. Total rock stars busting their asses. And the stuff we're shooting. My God. I can't wait for you to see it. I go back in about 8 hours to do more. I am doing what I love. It doesn't feel like work. Even though it is. I'm having fun. I'm overcome with joy and gratitude. I felt like posting this to say to anyone out there chasing your dream…Fifteen years ago I felt the same passion I feel today, but I had very little opportunity. I had to hustle hard and go hungry. I had to eat sardines and figure out how to get gas money. And I never had a plan B. I never stopped believing. Ever. Don't give up. Apply constant pressure for as long as it takes. It will break before you do. Go get it.

When it comes to success, there is always vacancy for those who hustle. Yes, it is hard work, but the rewards are worth it. You get what you go for, so start going for it!

*"Make sure when you wake up in the morning
that you know you accomplished everything you possibly
could the previous day. And then do it again!"*

— Ray Bradbury

SOUVENIR STOP

I AM GOING TO GIVE you a lot of takeaways in this Souvenir Stop. Thirty inspirational/motivational quotes about work and hustle that you can use every day for the next month. My approach for this Souvenir Stop is inspired by Jon Acuff's *30 Days of Hustle* and Walt Disney World's Fastpass+ System—a system that allows you to reserve your Fastpass attractions thirty days in advance of your visit. We now know that we will have to both work and wait for our dream, but who couldn't use a Fastpass or two along the way?

Day 1: *"I've never known Walt when he wasn't working."*
— Roy Disney

Day 2: *"The dream is free, but the hustle is sold separately."*
— Anonymous

Day 3: *"I never dreamed about success. I worked for it."*
— Estée Lauder

Day 4: *"The best kinds of people in your life aren't those who gather to celebrate your success, but those who gather to help your hustle."*
— Usman Ismaheel

Day 5: *"Life is short. Don't be lazy."*
— Sophia Amoruso

Day 6: *"You can't have a million-dollar dream with a minimum-wage work ethic."*
— Stephen C. Hogan

Day 7: *"The amount of good luck coming your way depends on your willingness to act."*

— Barbara Sher

Day 8: *"Luck is a word lazy people use to describe people who are hustling."*

— Jon Acuff

Day 9: *"Today I will do what others won't, so tomorrow I can do what others can't."*

— Jerry Rice

Day 10: *"We know we cannot hit a home run with the bases loaded every time we go to the plate. We also know the only way we can even get to first base is by constantly going to bat and continuing to swing."*

— Walt Disney

Day 11: *"Talent is cheaper than table salt. What separates the talented individual from the successful one is a lot of hard work."*

— Stephen King

Day 12: *"I've got a dream that's worth more than my sleep."*

— Eric Thomas

Day 13: *"Hustle beats talent when talent doesn't hustle."*

— Ross Simmonds

Day 14: *"Look in the mirror. That's your competition."*

— Anonymous

Day 15: *"We have a business here we built from scratch and, boy, we had to scratch plenty."*

— Walt Disney

Day 16: *"The best work requires the willingness to go the extra mile even after you feel that you've just completed a marathon—to exceed what you consciously believe is possible."*

— Michael Eisner

Day 17: *"Some succeed because they are destined to. But most succeed because they are determined to."*

— Henry Van Dyke

Day 18: *"Hustle isn't just working on the things you like. It means doing the things you don't enjoy so you can do the things you love."*

— Anonymous

Day 19: *"Constant motion delivers life-changing results. So focus on the constant motion part, not the destination part."*

— Jesse Tevelow

Day 20: *"I'd rather hustle 24/7 than slave 9 to 5."*

— Anonymous

Day 21: *"Hustle in silence and let your success make the noise."*

— Anonymous

Day 22: *"Those at the top of the mountain didn't fall there."*

— Marcus Washling

Day 23: *"The doors will be opened to those bold enough to knock."*

— Tony Gaskins

Day 24: *"Hustle until you no longer need to introduce yourself."*

— Anonymous

Day 25: *"The trouble with opportunity is that it always comes disguised as hard work."*

— Herbert V. Prochnow

Day 26: *"Who needs institutional authorities when you can hustle instead?"*

— Jesse Tevelow

Day 27: *"Don't be upset with the results you didn't get from the work you didn't do."*

— Anonymous

Day 28: *"You don't get what you wish for; you get what you work for."*

— Anonymous

Day 29: *"Do or do not; there is no try."*

— Yoda

Day 30: *"Invent your own job; take such an interest in it that you eat, sleep, dream, walk, talk, and live nothing but your work until you succeed."*

— Walt Disney

GETTING YOUR HAND STAMPED

DICK NUNIS WAS AN ACADEMIC All-American football player at USC with prospects of a promising, pro career until a broken neck shattered his second season. Instead of going to the NFL, Nunis graduated with a degree in education and then started working at Disneyland during its inaugural summer of 1955.

Van Arsdale France, the man responsible for founding Disney University—Disneyland's orientation and training program—hired Dick to be his "gofer," a newly hired person asked by superiors to "go for" this or that. Together, Dick and Van Arsdale France wrote the book on what it means to work at Disneyland.

Thanks to his tireless work ethic and willingness to hustle, Dick Nunis, aka the "White Tornado," turned his summer job into a full-time career. Over the next four decades, Dick worked as an area supervisor, supervisor of the mailroom and steno pool, director of Disneyland operations, vice president of Disneyland operations, and eventually executive vice president and then president of both Disneyland and Walt Disney World.

In May 1971, Walt Disney World was in trouble. Construction was at a crawl, and getting everything finished in a mere five months looked like an impossibility. "If the Magic Kingdom was to open on time, a hard-driving, single-minded general was needed on site, day and night." The company called on Dick Nunis, the man at Disneyland famous for getting things done. In *Realityland,* David Koenig tell us that Dick agreed to relocate temporarily to Florida on one condition: "When I call California needing something, it means yesterday."

Aside from his bark, Nunis was also known as a boss who "never asks anyone to do anything he wouldn't do himself. He doesn't sit behind a desk and think it will happen." As the months before opening in Florida melted down to weeks, then days, then hours, then minutes, the "White Tornado" managed to maintain his reputation as someone who would "roll up his sleeves and start working alongside them, to set a pace." In *Secret Stories of Walt Disney World*, Korkis gives us an example from Nunis' behavior the night before opening:

> On Thursday, September 30, 1971, the Contemporary Resort looked austere as it rose above the empty landscape. There was no grass, no bushes or trees to be seen. Dick Nunis took charge and shortly before 5 p.m., about fifteen hours before the Magic Kingdom would open to guests for the first time, Nunis began directing like a general a ragtag troop of college students, cast members, and some unskilled workers.

Disney landscaper Bill Evans recalled:

> Planting a few palm trees would be no problem, but we also figured it would take about four-and-a-half acres of sod just to make the place look presentable. Given the timetable, most everyone thought it an impossible task. Everyone but Nunis. He made the calls to have the sod trucked in, hired about a hundred extra men, none of whom knew anything about laying sod, grabbed anybody else that was standing around, and began turning the brown earth green.

It grew dark as the precious hours ticked by and the workers lugged heavy clumps of grass across the vast expanse. However, for decades, the one thing that people remembered about that night was Nunis in a loud and hoarse voice proclaiming, "Green side up! Remember, green side up!"

By 6 a.m. the next morning, the Contemporary was ready for the guests and the Magic Kingdom opened on time.

In 1999, after forty-four years of tireless service to Disney, the "White Tornado" was finally ready to retire. Today, Dick Nunis is a Disney Legend.
Nice work, pal.

"People often ask me if I know the secret of success…
and could tell others how to make their dreams come true.
My answer is you do it by working."

— Walt Disney

OVERCOMING OBSTACLES

*"The brick walls are there for a reason. They're not
there to keep us out. The brick walls are there to give us
a chance to show how badly we want something."*

— Dr. Randy Pausch in *The Last Lecture*
University Professor and Disney Imagineer

ARE WE THERE YET?

BEFORE THEY EVER TURNED THE first spade of dirt, the designers of
Walt Disney World's Magic Kingdom intentionally set out to make a
grand first impression. Every first-time visitor makes note of this first
impression, but it is especially impressive for guests coming from the
West Coast who are accustomed to the smaller size, scale, and scope
of Disneyland.

For fans from Anaheim who make it a habit to spot Matterhorn
Mountain from the freeway, the reality that a forest fills the five-mile
buffer between the interstate and Florida's first theme park is a jaw-
dropping realization. You cannot appreciate the difference between
160 acres and 27,000 acres until you are driving—and driving—and
driving through them.

Pulling into the parking lot, you realize that the Magic Kingdom
is still two miles away, but the monorail is right there! It waits for you

at the Transportation and Ticket Center—not as an attraction like at
Disneyland but as an actual mode of transportation—just like Walt
wanted all those many years ago. As you board the train and embark
on your journey through the "highway in the sky," you realize you can
see not only the entrance to the Magic Kingdom across the beautiful
Seven Seas Lagoon but also the spires of Cinderella Castle towering
toward the sun. You still haven't stepped onto Main Street, and yet you
are already blown away by the presentation playing out in front of you.

What few guests realize is that this presentation, a significant part
of the memorable show as you make your way to the Magic Kingdom
at Walt Disney World, wasn't necessarily a part of the original design.
No, Seven Seas Lagoon, the beautiful body of water that makes all this
possible, sits where the parking lot was intended to be.

What happened?

The same thing that happens with every dream. You start thinking
you are going to work in one direction only to discover that obstacles
require you to go in a direction you never intended or imagined. Bay
Lake, the beautiful body of water that sits between the Contemporary
Resort and Magic Kingdom, is what attracted Walt to this specific tract
of swamp. In 1966, the year that he died, Walt made a rudimentary
sketch of where he *thought* things should go in Florida. This basic
drawing—which included spots for the first theme park, resort hotels,
lake, and campgrounds—became the basic model that Disney followed
in Florida even after Walt's death.

Necessary air and grounds studies, more exact than Walt's original
sketch, revealed that some of the land was high ground and ideal for
construction while other sections were too low, even with extensive
fill, and thus, unsuitable for construction. Instead of giving up, Disney
decided to turn what appeared to be an obstacle into an *opportunity*.
Stephanie Barczewski explains further in *Magic Kingdoms: A History
of the Disney Theme Parks*, "[T]he land in front of the proposed site
for the Magic Kingdom contained an unpleasant [surprise]: it was
too swampy to support a parking lot. Disney turned necessity into

invention, and decided to create a second water feature, the Seven Seas Lagoon, in front of the Magic Kingdom. This made the entrance to the theme park more visually appealing and fully isolated it from the 'real world,' as Walt had wanted."

> *"I never cease to wonder how the thing [Walt Disney World] ever got built in the first place."*
>
> — Jeff Kurti

THE OBSTACLE IN THE PATH

IF YOU WANT TO EXPERIENCE a true sense of success, then you must learn to overcome your obstacles. The second you start working on a dream, the second you start leading rather than managing, the second you stop standing still and start taking your life to another level, obstacles are going to appear out of nowhere and everywhere. This is a sign that you are on the right path. Why? Because according to an ancient Zen story, recounted in Ryan Holiday's *The Obstacle Is the Way*, the obstacle in the path *is* the Path. The story goes like this:

There was once a king that believed his kingdom could be on the decline as a result of the attitude of his people. To prove his theory that his people had lost inspiration, a king had a giant boulder placed on the only road into this city. Then, hidden and perched on a hill, he waited to see what would happen.

First, some merchants came upon the rock and said, "Well, this boulder is blocking our path. Let's turn around and go home. No work today!" And they turned around and left. Next a group of soldiers came upon the boulder. "This rock is blocking our path," they said. "I guess no one will need our services today", and they turned around and went home as well.

The king watched person after person continue to come upon the rock, see it as an impasse or excuse and turn and go home. That was, until an old man came upon the rock. Instead of becoming discouraged like the others, he got excited by the presence of such a challenge. He first examined the huge boulder and tried to push it with all his might. He realized this would not work and began to think of other solutions. Then the quote from ancient mathematician Archimedes popped into his head, "If you give me a large enough lever and a fulcrum on which to place it, I shall move the world."

The old man was instantly inspired, and found a long wooden pole. He placed the pole under the boulder and using leverage, moved the boulder slightly. He repeated this process until the boulder was completely off the road. With his challenge finished, the inspired man was about to set off down the previously blocked path toward the city, but he noticed a bag lying where the boulder once stood. He looked around, picked up the bag and found inside a large amount of gold and a note. He carefully opened the note and read, "This gold is for you, since you know that great obstacles can lead to bigger opportunities."

The king, happy with the actions of this man, left his hiding place and went back to his castle with hope for his people.

It is tempting to want life—including our dreams and successes—to be easy and carefree. But every day can't be like a day at Disneyland—at least not when you're working to accomplish something meaningful and worthwhile. True riches are found when we learn to leverage what, at first glance, looks like an obstacle into a long-standing opportunity. Again, the obstacle in your path *is* the Path.

While you think about examples that prove this point in your life, allow me to share an example from mine. On Palm Sunday, 1989, I received an alarming late evening call. The church in Sonoma, California, where I was serving as pastor, was on fire. Originally, the building had served as a carriage house for the old Spreckles Sugar estate. It had been meticulously constructed with redwood and other fine materials that aren't even available to contractors today. The entire second floor was an old, open hayloft with hay chutes that served as ready-made chimneys into the Sunday School rooms (former horse stalls) down below. For years, the Sonoma Fire Marshall had warned us that if the building ever caught fire, it would be a total loss because there was no way firefighters could battle the blaze that would ensue.

Unfortunately, that day had finally come.

I raced from my apartment in Marin County, California, to the church property in Sonoma. Fifteen miles away, I could already see the flames shooting into the night sky. By the time I reached the parish property, our worst fears were confirmed. The structure, except for a St. Andrew style cross that the firemen had rescued from the building as it began to collapse in on itself, was a total loss. The good news was that no one was hurt, but as a congregation, we instantly became nomads in the wine country's Valley of the Moon.

Fire has an interesting way of cleansing things, even congregations. Before that night, we had a rather disparate demographic of believers, so we frequently found ourselves squabbling over the smallest matters of details and consequence. Should we have an early, more contemporary service, or a later, more traditional Sunday morning service? What are we going to do with the young people who keep showing up and are always too noisy, too rowdy, and too much "not like us"? How do we handle young families who insist on bringing children into the sanctuary rather than putting them in the church nursery where they "belong"?

Overnight, these obstacles disappeared. What had been a divided congregation was now a united church family focused on the singular goal of surviving and rebuilding. Looking back almost thirty years later, I am happy to report that the Palm Sunday Fire of 1989 was the *best* thing that ever happened to our church. It took three years to rebuild, but during that time, we ministered more and mattered more in the lives of our community than at any time before or after the fire. In 1992, we moved into a beautiful, architecturally award-winning facility that remains a beacon for believers in the heart of the California Wine Country. A facility made possible due to difficulties, adversity, and a seemingly overwhelming obstacle.

> *"It turned out that getting fired from Apple was the best thing that could have ever happened to me. The heaviness of being successful was replaced by the lightness of being a beginner again, less sure about everything. It freed me to enter one of the most creative periods of my life."*
>
> — Steve Jobs

WHAT WE REMEMBER

IT'S BEEN MORE THAN FIFTY years since Walt Disney's death. What we remember most are all of Walt's successes. These successes include the world's most popular cartoon character, Mickey Mouse; the world's first full-length animated feature film, *Snow White and the Seven Dwarfs*; and his dream, a dream called Disneyland.

What I fear, however, is that after all this time, the world has forgotten all of Walt's failures. We forget that Walt went bankrupt at age twenty-one. We forget that he lost his first successful cartoon character, Oswald the Lucky Rabbit, to Charles Mintz and his distributor, Universal. We forget that most of his movies *lost* money during their first theatrical run. We forget that his first dream for an amusement park, Mickey Mouse

Park, was planned for Burbank, but the Burbank City Council wanted nothing to do with Walt's dream—nothing to do with an amusement park; they didn't want a "carnival atmosphere" in their town.

Like most of us, Walt Disney wasn't born successful. After all his success, when it came to his dream of Disneyland, even Walt could not just speak the words "Magic Kingdom" and make his dream magically appear out of an orange grove in Anaheim. To see his dreams come true, Walt had to overcome the same sorts of obstacles and adversities we all face. Walt reminded us of this when, in 1947, he contributed the following essay to the book *Words to Live By*. Walt's words are as true today as they were more than seventy years ago.

TAKE A CHANCE
by
Walt Disney
Motion Picture Producer

"In the lexicon of youth...there is no such word as fail!"

— Edward Bulwer-Lytton

I wonder how many times these sturdy old words have been used in graduation speeches each year. They take me back to my own high school days, when I had my first pair of white flannel trousers and the world ahead held no heartbreak or fear.

Certainly, we have all had this confidence at one time in our lives, though most of us lose it as we grow older. Perhaps, because of my work, I've been lucky enough to retain a shred of this youthful quality. But sometimes, as I look back on how tough things were, I wonder if I'd go through it again. I hope I would.

When I was about twenty-one, I went broke for the first time. I slept on chair cushions in my "studio" in Kansas City and ate cold beans out of a can. But I took another look at my dream and set out for Hollywood.

Foolish? Not to a youngster. An older person might have had too much "common sense" to do it. Sometimes I wonder if "common sense" isn't another way of saying "fear." And "fear" too often spells failure.

In the lexicon of youth there is no such word as "fail." Remember the story about the boy who wanted to march in the circus parade? When the show came to town, the bandmaster needed a trombonist, so the boy signed up. He hadn't marched a block before the fearful noises from his horn caused two old ladies to faint and a horse to run away. The bandmaster demanded, "Why didn't you tell me you couldn't play the trombone?" And the boy said, "How did I know? I never tried before!"

Many years ago, I might have done just what that boy did. Now I'm a grandfather and have a good many gray hairs and what a lot of people would call common sense. But if I'm no longer young in age, I hope I stay young enough in spirit to never fear failure—young enough still to take a chance and march in the parade.

THE 25 PERCENT REPORT

When I started my career in higher education, nearly two decades ago, I jumped in with both feet working as both an administrator and a full-time faculty member. I enjoy both roles, but teaching comes more naturally to me than administration.

As a campus dean, I was required to complete a "25 percent report" which recorded, for accreditation purposes, the number of faculty who were teaching with doctorate degrees versus those with master's degrees each semester at our Arizona campus. I cringe at the word "report," and given my pathetic math skills, I was 100 percent certain that I would screw up the 25 percent report and risk our campus' ability to keep teaching and possibly the school's entire accreditation.

The solution?

Nothing.

Sure, I thought about it every now and again. But I knew I had no idea how to complete the darn thing. No one had yet asked me about it, so I stayed stuck in the security of knowing I didn't know *how* to do the report and that would be my go-to excuse when the time came.

After two-and-a-half semesters, the time finally came. One morning, my boss at the main campus some 1,000 miles away called me and said, "Barnes, I understand you are on your third semester there in Arizona, but your campus has yet to complete the required 25 percent report. What's going on down there?"

"Well, sir," I stammered. "I've, um, heard of the 25 percent report. I know that it is important and needs to be done. But you see, this is still my first year and I'm learning the job. The reason I haven't done it is because I don't know how."

"Barnes, I know this is your first year, but you are already on your third semester. I tell you what; you figure out *how* to complete the 25 percent report and get it to me by the end of the day, *or* I can hire a different dean who already knows how to do it."

Guess what? I figured out how to complete the 25 percent report and had three of them submitted by the end of the day.

One of the biggest obstacles to our dreams and our success is that we spend far too much time thinking and worrying about "how." The "how" then becomes an obstacle because if we knew "how," then we no doubt would have done it already. Instead, the better strategy is to focus on the "why."

Why?

Because once you have a big enough "why," your "how" will naturally follow. After getting off the phone with my boss, I still had no clue how to complete the required report. How was I able to figure it all out in less than a day after all those many months?

Simple.

I wanted to keep my job. That "why" gave me more than enough motivation to overcome the "how" supposedly standing in my way. Today I am happy to report that success is 99 percent "why" and only 1 percent "how."

THE WORLD IS YOUR OBSTACLE

MY AND NIKI'S FAVORITE THING to do when visiting Florida is to take an evening stroll around Epcot's World Showcase Lagoon. We are surrounded by water on one side and an array of international stores, shows, culture, and cuisine on the other. Unlike the frenetic, Fastpass pace of other Disney parks, which are attraction-centric, World Showcase is wholly about the setting.

And the setting is perfect.

Amid that scene, one can almost believe, for just a moment, that World Showcase has always been there.

This is how the world is.

This is how the world always has been.

This is how the world always will be.

Of course, World Showcase has *not* always been there. In fact, how Disney employees willed the back half of Epcot into existence provides us with examples of overcoming obstacles so outrageous that even the Disney studio hasn't dared turn these stories into another far-fetched, Hollywood fantasy film. Excerpts include:

Philippines Pavilion—The Philippines represents Disney's first attempt to present the concept of World Showcase overseas. After a harrowing flight across the Pacific, Philippine Airlines lost the Disney representatives' luggage. The team then waited twelve days for an eight-minute meeting with Mrs. Imelda Marcos where the woman, famous for having more than 2,500 pairs of shoes, stated "our people have no power and no money." The Philippine Pavilion was never built.

Mexico Pavilion—The model for the Mexico Pavilion was swapped during shipping for a coffin that was complete with a corpse destined for Guatemala. Disney dignitaries located the model and then drove to the scheduled meeting they were supposed to have with Mexico's Secretary of the Ministry of Tourism. Because the elevator was out of service, they had to haul the model up five flights of stairs. Once there, they learned the secretary had gone skiing in Colorado and would not return for two days. Two days later, the Disney representatives waited more than six hours, but the secretary never showed. Artwork associated with the model was also lost at the airport, but eventually, it was recovered—in a million pieces. Disney was successful in selling Mexico on World Showcase but only after waiting another four hours for the secretary to show, and only then by showing a highlight film on a bedsheet that had to be tacked to a wall to serve as a movie screen.

Iranian Pavilion—Disney's meetings in Iran to sell World Showcase took place in 1978, one year before the Iranian Revolution. The shah was still in power, but like the secretary in Mexico, when the Disney team members arrived for their meeting with the country's leader, it learned that he, too, had gone skiing—in Switzerland. Over time, one member of the Disney team fell madly in love with the shahbanu—the First Lady of Iran and the Shah's wife. This was *not* "a whole new world," however, so nothing ever came of that relationship. After the Disney team members stayed in the city for more than six weeks and only ever ate dinner in their hotel rooms due to security concerns, this same would-be Romeo nearly died from a severe case of gastritis that a local doctor treated with pills filled with pure, uncut heroin.

Moroccan Pavilion—The wait between the initial meeting in Morocco and a follow-up meeting was more than eighteen months. In the interim, the Disney delegation decided to leave the intricate

Moroccan model behind. Upon their return, they learned that the ten-year old prince of Morocco had turned the model into a beloved toy—complete with an electric train. Their efforts to retrieve the model were met with a literal, royal hissy-fit and threats of beheading.

> *"A lot of people don't realize that we have some very serious problems here, keepin' this thing going and gettin' it started. I remember when we opened [Disneyland], if anybody recalls, we didn't have enough money to finish the landscaping and I had Bill Evans go out and put Latin tags on all the weeds."*
>
> — Walt Disney

BABY, THERE'S MOLD INSIDE!

THE OBSTACLES ARE NEVER GOING to end. You are always either in a crisis, coming out of a crisis, or going into a crisis. This is the cycle of life, and it never stops and it never ends. As I write this, a few days before Christmas, I am having to deal with the news that our kitchen is flooded. It started a few nights ago with what we thought was a simple drain clog. I poured some drain cleaner into the sink, the water started flowing, and problem was solved—or so I thought. When the sink continued to clog, we finally relented and called a plumber. Soon enough, we discovered that the problem is much more extensive and that water has been running inside our walls, underneath our floor, and outside onto our patio for a full three days. In the background, I can hear the whirrs of the fans trying to dry everything out before a final assessment is made regarding the presence of mold and exactly how much will need to be ripped out to restore everything to working order.

This is *not* what I had planned for the holidays. Sometimes you feel helpless to what feels like the fickleness of life. You are going strong in one direction and then, BAM, something unexpected hits you and you find yourself veering off into a course you never wanted to go. I want to use the plumbing as an excuse to be pathetic. I want to use the water as an excuse not to write. I want to use the damage as a reason for doing self-inflicted damage to my own dreams and my own goals. If life is really this capricious, then what is the point? It seems impossible ever to get ahead. We will always struggle upstream—unable to make headway and genuinely move forward.

But that's a lie. Regardless of whether I quit or whether I write, the water will still be there. I can't control what happens next, but I can control what I do next. In other words, my response to an obstacle is my responsibility.

> *"Dealing with the temporary frustration of not making progress is an integral part of the path towards excellence.... If the pursuit of excellence was easy, everyone would do it. In fact, this impatience in dealing with frustration is the primary reason that most people fail to achieve their goals."*

> — Christopher Sommer

SOUVENIR STOP

LOOK FOR LEVERAGE—EVERYTHING YOU ARE facing today is either an obstacle *or* an opportunity. The only difference between the two is the meaning *you* attach—and the meaning you attach will either empower you or disable you. Either way, the choice is up to you.

To help put this in perspective, take a moment to reflect on past obstacles you have overcome and how those situations have helped make you who you are today. An example for me comes from being grounded from riding my favorite Disney rides for twenty-four months while I recovered from brain surgery in 2014. Was I happy about it?

No, of course not! But I used that time to fulfill my dream of writing *The Wisdom of Walt*. A good trade!

Your Past Experience(s) with Obstacles:

_____
_____
_____

How You Benefited:

_____
_____
_____

Your Current Obstacle:

_____
_____
_____

How Can You Leverage Your Obstacle into an Opportunity?

_____
_____
_____

> *"What if every problem and pain you had was life happening for you—not to you?"*
>
> — Tony Robbins

GET GRITTY—WHEN IT COMES TO success, talent and passion are important, but your ability to persevere is paramount. It is one thing to set goals, but it is something else to stick to those goals in the face of all obstacles.

Angela Duckworth, Professor of Psychology at the University of Pennsylvania, has spent her career studying and measuring "grit." She believes that having stamina, a willingness to stick with your goals for the future—day in and day out—is the determining factor between those who achieve their goals and those who do not. Interested in finding out just how "gritty" you are? Then take this quiz: https:// angeladuckworth.com/grit-scale/

"If our young men miscarry in their first enterprises, they lose all heart. If the young merchant fails, men say he is ruined. If the finest genius studies at one of our colleges, and is not installed in an office within one year afterwards in the cities or suburbs of Boston or New York, it seems to his friends and to himself that he is right in being disheartened, and in complaining the rest of his life."

— Ralph Waldo Emerson, written in 1841

REMEMBER WHY—IF SUCCESS REALLY IS 99 percent why and only 1 percent how, let's use this space to focus on your "why."
Explore the following questions:

1. Why does your dream matter to you?

_____

_____

_____

_____

2. Why will your dream, once accomplished, matter to others?

_____

_____

_____

_____

3. Knowing that obstacles are inevitable, and more are on their way, why are you willing to persevere?

_____

_____

_____

"It's okay to get discouraged. It's not okay to quit."

— Ryan Holiday

GETTING YOUR HAND STAMPED

ONE OF THE MOST FAMOUS features of Walt Disney World's Magic Kingdom is the famed underground "utilidors." The utilidors, a combination of the words "utility" and "corridor," are the byproduct of an early story from Disneyland. Walt was horrified one day when he witnessed a cast member, dressed as a cowboy for Frontierland, walking through Tomorrowland on his way to work. Walt's thoughts went something like this:

There goes the illusion.

There goes the magic.

There goes the story.

For Florida, Walt envisioned a subterranean network of tunnels and offices as the solution to telling stories *and* maintaining the magic. By placing all park operations underground, necessary support services would be out of sight.

The obstacle?

The water table in Florida is high. In Central Florida, it is *very* high. You can't go digging without soon hitting a deluge of water. The Imagineers engineered a solution by building Walt's subterranean support system *above* ground. How?

Remember the Seven Seas Lagoon at the start of our chapter? Yes, the same lagoon that started out as a parking lot but, out of necessity, was transformed into a man-made body of water? In creating the Seven Seas Lagoon, engineers dredged nine million cubic yards of earth and repurposed it to raise the site of Magic Kingdom by fourteen feet. In other words, the utilidors are *not* underground but at ground level. The Magic Kingdom, the part of the park that you and I experience and enjoy, is one level up. Just as Walt envisioned it, everything necessary for making the magic—from waste removal to cutting cast members' hair—is done down below.

How do we overcome obstacles?

By recognizing that the obstacle in the path *is* the path.

Today, whatever stands between you and your dream is there for a reason. Stop asking "why" the obstacle is there and start asking "how." How can you use this obstacle to your benefit? How can you leverage this obstacle to take your dream and your success to the next level?

Speaking of levels, raising the Magic Kingdom to the second level provided the added benefit of making it more visible and impressive from across the lagoon. Digging deeper, beneath the swampy muck of what became Seven Seas Lagoon, Disney discovered beautiful, pristine white sand.

Today, you can celebrate your success by sinking your toes into the sand on the beaches that surround the Contemporary, Polynesian, and Grand Floridian Resorts. Sand discovered because of Disney's willingness to overcome obstacles.

> *"The problem is not the problem; the problem is your attitude about the problem."*
>
> — Captain Jack Sparrow

DEALING WITH DOUBTERS

"The truth of the matter is that by the time we had the studio built, the banks owed me money, thanks to Snow White. And it gave me more personal satisfaction than anything I have ever done because it proved to a lot of sneering critics that a full-length cartoon could make money."

— Walt Disney

FLYING HIGH

YOU MAY HAVE NEVER HEARD of her, but Tiny Kline is more than a tiny footnote in Disneyland's history. In 1961, Tiny started playing the part of Tinker Bell. She didn't do the role as a voiceover in an animated movie or play the pixie in a live-action film. No, Tiny is the Hungarian-born circus performer who, at the age of seventy, first soared over Sleeping Beauty Castle as part of the nightly "Fantasy in the Sky" fireworks show.

The making of Matterhorn Mountain in 1959 is what made the stunt possible in 1961. At 147 feet, the Matterhorn at Disneyland is a 1/100th replica of the original in Switzerland, yet (or *yeti*) still seventy feet taller than the adjacent castle just a few yards away. Each night, Tiny took to the top of the Matterhorn so she could descend a cable suspended over Sleeping Beauty Castle. Disney Legend Bill Sullivan

DEALING WITH DOUBTERS   125

(Sully), who started his career at Disneyland as a Jungle Cruise Skipper in 1955, tells us what would happen next in his book *From Jungle Cruise Skipper to Disney Legend*:

> We had big old football players at the catch tower where she'd land and she'd hit that thing just as fast as she could and BAM, she'd knock these guys over and she'd go, 'Thank you, boys!'
>
> She'd get up as if nothing had happened. She loved to hit those two mattresses. The harder she hit, the better she liked it.

"Sully" moved to Orlando in 1969 to become one of the many Disneyland cast members tasked with translating the magic of Disneyland to Walt Disney World's Magic Kingdom. As the park's Vice President, he always dreamed of having Tinker Bell fly over Cinderella Castle just as she flew over Sleeping Beauty Castle at Disneyland. "A good idea is a good idea, and we found that if people liked it in Disneyland, they liked it in Magic Kingdom, too." This was no tiny task, however, because at 189 feet, Cinderella Castle is nearly three times the size of Disneyland's castle *and* there is no Matterhorn Mountain from which to launch. Everyone doubted it could be done, but those doubts didn't sully Sullivan's dream.

Invigorated by the new and imaginative leadership of Michael Eisner and Frank Wells, Sullivan and two other Disneylanders, Hank Daines and Arnold Lindbergh, vowed at a company Christmas party in 1984 that they would finally find a way to make Tinker Bell fly in Florida. With an initial budget of $25,000 that soon soared to $250,000, Sullivan rebuilt the top spire of Cinderella Castle, conducted line tests with sandbags and mannequins, hooked a line running from the castle's spire to the top of If You Had Wings in nearby Tomorrowland, and hired acrobatic circus performers from nearby Circus World. With everything in place, it was show time…time to show the doubters that it could be done. David Koenig shares the story in *Realityland*:

> Sullivan knew Eisner and Wells would be in town for the Fourth of July, so he scheduled the first unadvertised performance for that Night, to introduce the holiday fireworks show. Just as the show was about to begin, spotlights circled the sky, then converged on a tiny figure in sparkling green, 165 feet up, at the top of the castle. The crowd gasped as the pixie swooped down from the golden spire, smiling and waving as she sailed over the Plaza, before disappearing into the darkness. Eisner and Wells' jaws dropped.

People who start chasing their dreams eventually get chased by doubters. When you start flying high, you must be prepared for those who wish to bring you down. Like Tiny hitting the mattresses in Tinker Bell's catch tower, you will get hit by haters. And if you are not careful, BAM, you and your dream will soon be grounded.

> *"In the end, people will judge you anyway, so don't live your life impressing others, live your life impressing yourself."*
>
> — Eunice Camacho Infanta

YOU ARE NOT ALONE

Do you have doubters in your life? People who don't believe in you? People who don't believe in your ideas, your crazy thoughts, your dreams?

You are not alone.

Walt Disney spent his entire life dealing with doubters, and it wasn't just Disneyland that brought out the naysayers and the ne'er-do-wells.

From Walt's earliest years, people scoffed at his skills and questioned what contribution he could ever possibly make to the world. His father, Elias, was especially harsh and often rebuked Walt for "wasting time" drawing pictures. Time, in Elias' opinion, that could be far better spent finishing farm chores or school work. According to Walt himself in *How to Be Like Walt,* "[H]e just scoffed at me…and said that if I was foolish enough to want to become an artist, I should learn the violin. Then I could always get a job in a band if I was in need of money."

You would think that Walt's success with Mickey Mouse *and* the world's first full-length animated feature film, *Snow White and the Seven Dwarfs,* ended his dad's doubts. They didn't. After pouring the enormous profits from *Snow White* into building a new, state-of-the art animation studio in Burbank, California, Walt invited his father to take a tour of the nearly completed facility at 500 S. Buena Vista Street. Pat Williams and Jim Denney talk about this tour in *How to Be Like Walt:*

> It was an impressive complex of buildings, linked by underground tunnels (a precursor to the Magic Kingdom's utilidor tunnels), with extra-wide corridors and spacious offices, studios and stages. The buildings were surrounded by broad lawns and recreation spaces for volleyball, softball and badminton. Finally, Elias said, "But Walter, what can all this be used for?"
>
> "It's a movie studio, Dad," Walt replied. "It's the studio where I'll make my cartoons and feature films." Elias shook his head. "No Walt. I mean—what can it be *used* for?"
>
> Then Walt understood. His father wanted to know if the studio buildings had some "practical" use. Elias Disney never understood Walt's business, and he never would.

Walt sighed. "Well," he said, "if we decided to close the studio, this place would make a perfect hospital." As Walt guided his father around the studio, he didn't say another word about cartoons or feature films. "I went through the whole darn studio," he later recalled, "and I explained the thing to him as a hospital. And he was happy."

*"Great spirits have always encountered violent
opposition from mediocre minds."*

— Albert Einstein

IF YOU CAN MAKE IT IN NEW YORK

THIS PATTERN REPEATED ITSELF WITH Disneyland, and it is what drove Walt to expand east. After proving his doubters wrong with the success of Disneyland, Walt wanted to prove himself all over again to a different audience of skeptics and sneering critics. Walt knew that it was one thing to succeed with an amusement park in California, but what would it look like if he took his act on the road, east of the Mississippi and into New York City, the so-called Big Apple, and home to America's most sophisticated tastes and audiences? As David Koenig writes in *Realityland*:

> Walt was acutely aware that nearly two thirds of Disneyland's visitors came from California; in fact, only eight percent came from east of the Mississippi River. When Disneyland first opened, the entertainment and financial press from the East Coast couldn't understand it. Why would Walt waste millions of dollars turning orange groves into a circus?
>
> "The eastern media just totally pooh-poohed [Disneyland]," said the park's first marketing chief, Jack Lindquist. "It was

the old Lalaland routine: 'We're too sophisticated. It'll never fly here.'"

Before finding out how his park plans would fly in Florida, Walt first had the chance to test his new market in New York. At the 1964-65 World's Fair, Walt and his Imagineers constructed attractions for four pavilions: *The Ford Magic Skyway, Progressland (Carousel of Progress), Great Moments with Mr. Lincoln,* and *"it's a small world."* According to Sam Gennawey in *Walt Disney and the Promise of Progress City,* "The Disney pavilions were a smash hit, and Walt realized that his style of entertainment would work with the 'sophisticated' northeast crowd."

The greatest risk Walt took in New York was with Great Moments with Mr. Lincoln. The world's first Audio-Animatronics attraction, Walt Disney's Enchanted Tiki Room, had opened only one year earlier. Now Walt was attempting to construct the world's first human Audio-Animatronics figure. It was Robert Moses, the powerful New York bureaucrat and head of the 1964-65 fair, who insisted that Abe be an attraction in New York. According to the Walt Disney Family Museum, "Walt brought Moses in to 'meet' Lincoln, and when the robotic president extended his hand, Moses was dumbfounded. 'I won't open the fair without that exhibit!' he exclaimed."

In agreeing to do the show, Walt opened himself up to an array of criticism. Aside from the technological challenges, many were opposed to the idea that Disney dared to bring one of America's most revered presidents back to life in such an artificial and disrespectful manner. It is one thing to bring birds to life. But a person, let alone a president? How dare Walt Disney play God!

Yet it is Great Moments with Mr. Lincoln that is the direct link to the revered, opening day attraction in Magic Kingdom's Liberty Square. Hall of Presidents represents Walt's original vision for Great Moments with Mr. Lincoln. From the beginning, Walt wanted an area in Disneyland that honored *every* American President. He couldn't find a way to pay for it, however, until Moses made certain that Lincoln be a part of the 1964-65 World's Fair. After the fair, Lincoln found a home at the Main Street Opera House in Disneyland, and later that decade, Imagineers got busy building the fully realized version for Florida.

Hall of Presidents is housed in a building that resembles Philadelphia's Independence Hall and, per an Act of Congress, is home to the only permanent Presidential Seal outside of The White House. Here we hear not from just one president, but via roll call from every president. A select few even give speeches. In the *spirit* of Great Moments with Mr. Lincoln and Hall of Presidents, let's take a moment to listen to one of our presidents.

Shhhhhh.

New York's own, former US President Theodore Roosevelt, is rising to speak:

> It is not the critic who counts; not the man who points out how the strong man stumbles, or where the doer of deeds could have done them better. The credit belongs to the man who is actually in the arena, whose face is marred by dust and sweat and blood; who strives valiantly; who errs, who comes short again and again, because there is no effort without error and shortcoming; but who does actually strive to do the deeds; who knows great enthusiasms, the great devotions; who spends himself in a worthy cause; who at the best knows in the end the triumph of high achievement, and who at the worst, if he fails, at least fails while daring greatly, so that his place shall never be with those cold and timid souls who neither know victory nor defeat.

The next time you are dealing with contrarian critics, remember "The Man in the Arena" speech. It reminds us that those taking shots can only take aim at those of us taking a chance.

*"The biggest mistake you can make is listening to people
who've given up on their dreams telling you to give up on
yours."*

— Umair Hague

THE FULL MONTE, CRISTO

WHEN I TOOK NIKI TO Disneyland on our honeymoon, her first
trip to The Happiest Place on Earth, she was skeptical that going
to an amusement park for our honeymoon would be able to keep
us entertained for five full days. Like the railroad that runs around
the perimeter of the park, she came full circle by the end of our first
evening. Now she wanted to know why we were *only* spending five
days at Disneyland!

Yet her doubts lingered regarding other experiences throughout
the week. For example, I made lunch reservations at the Blue Bayou
restaurant the afternoon of our first full day. I told Niki ahead of time
that this was the best restaurant anywhere in the resort.

"Right," she replied.

Niki has a degree in Culinary Arts and loves food the way Walt
loved Mickey Mouse, so she had reservations about how a meal at an
amusement park could be anything worth raving about.

Recognizing it would be impossible to convince her in advance
about the food, I instead started selling her on the ambiance. *Surely, this
is where having the Magic Kingdom's own marketing materials memorized
will pay off,* I thought.

"Babe, we will be surrounding ourselves in the essence of New
Orleans as overhead strings of colorful balloon lanterns cast an
enchanting glow, dotting the darkness where crickets chirp, frogs
croak, and fireflies wink all while our eyes are constantly adjusting
to the perpetual twilight. You will be enthralled as passengers from
the Pirates of the Caribbean sail through the eatery on their way to a

swashbuckling voyage to a long-forgotten time and place when pirates wrought havoc on the high seas."

Niki rolled her eyes at me, a sure sign it was beyond time for me to stop. The only havoc being wreaked was on my own honeymoon. Dead men tell no tales, so if I was ever going to tell this tale in a book, then I needed to shut up already!

We arrived promptly for our 11:30 a.m. reservation and were seated first. Our table sat exactly where I had envisioned it—next to the water and centered on the bayou. Niki was indeed enthralled as she observed overhead a beyond-believable nighttime sky, at noon, on a warm August day in Southern California.

"Wow!" she exclaimed. "This place is incredible!"

Satisfied with my restaurant selection, Niki sat down to scour the menu. I informed her that she need not bother looking at the menu because she would no doubt want the famed Monte Cristo sandwich.

"What's that?" she asked.

"It's a deep-fried turkey, ham, and Swiss cheese sandwich. They serve it with jelly that you dip the sandwich into and it is *amazing*," I replied.

As I age, I find it more and more difficult to see things clearly in dimly lit places. Nonetheless, the turning of Niki's nose and the twisting of her face was far more pronounced than the bumps on a book translated in Braille. It was clear to me that Niki wanted *nothing* to do with the Monte Cristo. Instead, she opted for the crab cake while I ordered the Monte Cristo, looking forward to enjoying all four delicious pieces by myself.

When the server arrived and presented me with my Monte Cristo, Niki was stunned at how succulent my sandwich suddenly looked.

"Wow, that looks amazing! Would it be okay if I had just one bite?"

Knowing that marriage is about sharing and compromise, I happily handed my sandwich over to my bride.

And I never saw my sandwich again. Niki ate the full Monte Cristo sandwich. Despite her initial doubts, today, whenever we want a nice meal at Disneyland, we always make reservations at the Blue Bayou and we only ever order the Monte Cristo—a sandwich we happily share together.

"My best idea was to not accept my wife's negative reaction when I asked her to marry me."

— Michael Eisner

YOU HAVE HEARD IT SAID, BUT NOW I TELL YOU....

BEING A "DISNEY HISTORIAN" ISN'T easy. First, there is no such thing, and second, you typically have to choose whether you are going to write for the scholars or write for the masses. I live in the vacuum of academics, but I dream big enough to trust that I can successfully navigate both arenas. My passion for believing that Walt and his parks can be the ultimate source of inspiration for all of us seeing our own dreams come true is what inspired me to teach a college course on The History of Disneyland—a class that can, at best, reach hundreds. This then transformed into the dream of writing a book, *The Wisdom of Walt*, that has reached thousands.

Like Walt, I have had to deal with my fair share of doubters along the way. Some try to scoff at my course. Others try to ballyhoo my book. When they are successful at neither, then I have to deal with naysayers who are more than happy to nitpick at any mistakes I might make along the way.

And I have made them.

I would love to tell you that *The Wisdom of Walt* has sold millions of copies. It hasn't. At least not yet. At the same time, I also haven't received the dozens of "cease and desist" letters from the Disney Company that many of my doubters predicted I would receive for daring to write a book about "Disney" without "permission." I tend to be an "it is easier to ask forgiveness than permission" kind of guy anyway, but I was also smart enough to reach out to individuals who have written other successful, and unauthorized, Disney books for advice and guidance along the way.

I would also love to tell you that *The Wisdom of Walt* is inerrant—perfect and without errors. I can't because it isn't. In fulfilling my dream of writing a book that uses Walt Disney and Disneyland to motivate and inspire others to pursue their own dreams, I made a few mistakes along the way. For example:

1. Each chapter begins with a quote from Walt Disney. Chapter One, "Sitting on a Park Bench," is supposed to set the example for all the chapters that follow. It opens with this Walt quote: "If you can dream it, you can do it." Here is the challenge. Walt *never* said, "If you can dream it, you can do it." As Disney historian Jim Korkis notes, "[I]t sure sounds like something Walt would say." In truth, these words belong to Imagineer Tom Fitzgerald, who created the quote for the exceptional 1983 attraction, Horizons. This is *not* the best way to start off a best-selling book!

2. In the first printing, there were several word errors that appeared relatively minor but added up over the course of the book. I claimed that Walt Disney was left-handed when, in fact, he was right-handed. I referred to Disneyland's opening day as "Black Friday" rather than "Black Sunday." I confused the various *Autopia* attractions that have appeared in the park over the years. I used the name Bay Lake when I meant the Seven Seas Lagoon. I referenced "it's a small world" as "It's a Small World," completely violating the spirit of this great attraction that seeks to capitalize on our greatest asset—our children.

A couple of critics were none too quick to point out the error of my ways and set me straight. I was comforted, however, by a reassuring email from Jim Korkis and the following words from his book *How to Be a Disney Historian:*

Keep a good sense of humor. Develop a thick skin against criticism and so-called experts who seek to diminish you or your work. You can get 499 things correct, many of them never before shared, and someone will still focus on the one that is misspelled, left out, or insist you should have written "Ubbe" rather than "Ub" when referring to Walt's first superstar animator.

Just like in the old movie Westerns, once you are known as the fastest gun, people will seek you out to challenge the title. You will never win. If you get something right, people will be unimpressed because you are supposed to know those things. If you get something wrong, people will be disappointed since you are supposed to know those things.

Try to ignore the haters. You will never change their minds. They may criticize you in public or behind your back on their Twitter feeds or Facebook posts. Trust that those people who do appreciate what you do may come to your defense.

PEOPLE SAY THE DARNDEST THINGS

ART LINKLETTER WAS A FRIEND to Walt Disney and a success in his own right. He was the host of numerous television shows, the author of twenty-three books, and aside from being the Master of Ceremonies for the opening day broadcast of Disneyland on ABC television on the afternoon of Sunday, July 17, he was probably most famous for his long-running series *Kids Say the Darndest Things*.

When Walt first took Art to Anaheim to show him where he would be building his dream called Disneyland, Art's immediate thought as they stood there amidst orange groves, walnut trees, bulldozers, and piles of dirt was "[M]y poor, deluded friend! He'll go broke!"

Fast forward a few years and Walt again approached Art. This time he wanted his opinion on purchasing thousands of acres in Florida, "enough land to do all the things I've ever dreamed of. I can build another Disneyland and have plenty of room for future projects. What do you think?"

Despite the success of Disneyland, Art's doubtful response mirrors his initial reaction to Walt's dream in the early 1950s. Here is Art Linkletter's version of the story as recounted in his own foreword to *How to Be Like Walt*:

> "Walt," I said, "when you first told me you were going to build Disneyland, I thought it was a terrible idea. Well, I was wrong then. But now, I think I've got some good advice for you: Don't do it. Don't build another Disneyland in Florida."
>
> He looked at me in dismay. "Why not?"
>
> "Look at what you've got over in Anaheim," I said. "Disneyland is one of a kind. It's like the Pyramids of Egypt or the Grand Canyon—there's nothing else like it in the world. As soon as you build another one, the original isn't unique anymore."

To Art's credit, years later he would go on to say that one of his biggest mistakes was not taking the opportunity to purchase real estate around Disneyland and, in doing so, passing up the chance to make millions. Regarding Florida, he would simply say, "[S]hows how much I knew!"

The real question here might not be, "What was Art thinking?" But rather "What was Walt thinking?" We know who the doubters in our lives are. We know who the naysayers can be. And yet we continue to insist on turning to those *exact same individuals* when it comes to advice, counsel, encouragement, enthusiasm, and validation for our own dreams.

SOUVENIR STOP

CRABS IN A BUCKET—DID YOU know that if you put a single crab in a bucket, the crab can easily escape on its own? However, if multiple crabs are present, no one escapes. Why? Because together, they keep grabbing each other and pulling down anyone attempting to make an escape.

We do the same with each other and our dreams. People who have given up on their dreams will do anything and everything possible to ensure that you don't achieve yours.

This isn't fair. Just a fact.

The crab, Sebastian, plays this part perfectly in *The Little Mermaid*. Remember when Ariel dreams of getting out from "under the sea" and being a "part of that world"? As much as Ariel wants her dreams to be more than just dreams, Sebastian, like "crabs in a bucket," spends most of the story trying to talk her out of taking risks and leaving the safety of the sea. Remember these words?

"Ariel, please! Will you get your head out of the clouds and back in the water where it belongs?"

"Ariel, listen to me. The human world is a mess. Life under the sea is better than anything they got up there."

"Somebody's got to nail that girl's fins to the floor."

Who are the people trying to pull you down? Rather than allowing their words to keep you grounded, I want to encourage you to use their words to remind you of where you are going versus where you are no longer willing to stay. Use the space below to write down the words others use to keep you safe *and* stuck.

Now, place those words in a prominent place and use them to remind yourself that you are going to *do* and *be* the exact opposite!

Right now, I have these words from a "friend" on my office wall. They aren't words of inspiration or motivation. Rather, they are words I use to fuel me to the next level in life.

"You are viewed as a person who is willing to break all sorts of limits and rules and move forward not caring what ramifications are left in your path."

DON'T RESIST THE RESISTANCE—DREAMS REQUIRE both courage and confidence. Courage to do something *big* and confidence to know you can make it happen. The resistance you will no doubt face can help you with both.

First, if everyone agrees with you and your dream, then by definition, you are not dreaming *big* enough. Secondly, confidence is a muscle. We grow our physical muscles via weight or *resistance* training. The way you grow your confidence muscle is by exposing your dream to as much resistance as possible. Your dream will become stronger as your confidence grows and you battle through the resistance of doubters, haters, and naysayers.

Which do you need more of? Courage or confidence. If it's courage, then how can you make your dream even bigger? If it's confidence, how can you use the resistance of others to build your confidence muscle bigger and make your dream stronger?

RESPECT THE ROLE—DREAMERS ARE PEOPLE who want to make new things happen. All doubters, however, aren't necessarily people who only desire to maintain the status quo. Aside from helping us grow our confidence, doubters can challenge our dreams and help us make the impractical, practical. The people who believe in us and who believe in our dreams can also have our best interests at heart when they question what we are doing or how we are going to do it. In other words, they can keep us from going down potentially dangerous paths.

I have several people in my life who play this role well. Niki doesn't always tell me what I want to hear, but she *always* tells me what I *need* to hear. My mother's maiden name was Pickett, and I am a direct descendant of General George Pickett—the same general who led the disastrous Pickett's charge—a loss that resulted in more than 6,000 casualties at Gettysburg and, some have argued, the Confederacy losing the Civil War.

The Union was right to win, and Niki is right to remind me of my heritage when I go charging head first—without considering the potential consequences or casualties.

Who do you trust to tell you the truth? Who is willing to tell you the truth even when you don't want to hear it?

GETTING YOUR HAND STAMPED

Just as Walt Disney World is home to multiple theme parks, this chapter's *Getting Your Hand Stamped* section is going to be home to multiple stories. Instead of park hopping, let's do some story hopping.

First, the relationship between Walt Disney and his older brother Roy was as paradoxical as that of the first famous pair of brothers, Cain and Abel. Only, in this instance, Roy *was* his brother's keeper. In an article touting Roy as Walt's best friend, Bill Ladonisi of wdwfacts. com notes that:

> [O]f all the characters, artisans, and friends that Walt Disney had amassed over his long, successful career, none was more important than his own brother, Roy O. Disney.... Despite being eight years older, he [Roy] doted on his little brother. He never minded watching over him, nor wheeling him around in the carriage.

But as the older brother, Roy could often take after his father when it came to doubting his little brother's dreams. Yes, it was Roy who encouraged Walt to join him in California, but it was also Roy who tried to discourage Walt from taking on the risk and expense of creating *Snow White and the Seven Dwarfs*. As the project progressed, Walt wanted valuable feedback from his studio team. Williams and Denny, in *How to Be Like Walt*, tell us what happened next:

> At one story conference, the animators, story artists, and other staffers filled out comment cards, detailing their ideas and suggestions about the story. The majority of comments were positive and enthusiastic—but one card read: "Walt, stick to shorts!"
>
> Walt was stunned. Someone in the studio was opposed to *Snow White*! Fuming, Walt invited the anonymous critic to meet him in his office, but no one stepped forward. The identity of the unknown critic became a matter of legend. Whenever Walt got irritated with one of his artists, he'd point an accusing finger and say, "You're the one who told me to stick to shorts!"
>
> Though Walt never learned who wrote that card, a handful of artists knew the identity of Walt's tormentor—and they delighted in keeping the secret.
>
> It was Walt's own brother, Roy.

Our second story comes twenty years later. Fast forward to the 1950s and Walt has another idea. Another crazy thought. Walt Disney has a dream. A dream called Disneyland. Roy is anything but enthusiastic, and the biggest obstacle between Walt and his dream for an amusement park is money. Roy holds the studio's purse strings—a purse that is still empty after years of losses during World War II. Worse, the studio is deep in debt to Bank of America. Working with the banks was Roy's responsibility, so anytime Walt went to the bank alone, Roy worried that Walt was off to pitch his "Mickey Mouse idea" for an amusement park.

At one point, Walt started raising money for Disneyland by collecting contributions from studio employees. Like a man selling Girl Scout cookies, Walt sold his dream $10 to $20 at a time. The group, led by studio nurse Hazel George, came to be known as the "Disneyland Backers and Boosters." The point wasn't to raise the $17 million that would one day be needed for Disneyland. Rather, the point was to needle Roy into reconsidering his opposition. According to Todd Pierce, author of *Three Years in Wonderland*, "[T]he employee investment strategy was really a ploy devised by Walt to cleverly shame Roy into the amusement park business."

The strategy worked.

Despite his initial opposition to "that damn amusement park" and his fears that Walt's latest fancy could bankrupt the studio the two had spent a lifetime together building, eventually Roy helped Walt find financing for the park via ABC television. By opening day, Walt's greatest critic was now his greatest convert. Who was the first person to spend the first dollar to purchase the first ticket to get into Disneyland?

It was Walt's own brother, Roy.

Our final story concerns when Walt was purchasing land for his final dream in Florida. He first purchased 12,000 acres—land that was already seventy-five times the size of Disneyland. The ever-conservative Roy believed this was more than adequate acreage for whatever his brother might have in mind for his next Magic Kingdom. Roy was, after all, the man who once believed land prices around Disneyland would *plummet* after the park opened. "Who in his right mind would want property next door to an amusement park?" Walt kept reminding Roy of his reservations with Disneyland, and so Roy kept writing checks until Walt had purchased more than 27,000 acres for Walt Disney World.

But before they could even break ground in Florida, the brother Roy had spent a lifetime protecting died. Instead of retiring as originally planned, Roy picked up the mantle and almost single-handedly willed his brother's final wish into fruition. What had started out as Project X, The Florida Project, EPCOT, or The East Coast Disneyland was now, on Roy's insistence, to be called Walt Disney World.

Today, when you walk into Walt Disney World's Magic Kingdom, you are greeted by a life-size bronze statue of a man perched on a park bench in Town Square. Sitting next to him is Mickey Mouse's lifelong partner, Minnie. The statue is a tribute to the man who gave the last years of his life to seeing Walt's last wish fulfilled and who himself died in December 1971, only two months after the Magic Kingdom opened.

It *is* Walt's own brother, Roy.

"Walt knew his ideas were good and the naysayers were wrong. Walt proved that the only way to get things done is by sticking to your ideas and your beliefs."

— Pat Williams and Jim Denney

FINANCING YOUR FUTURE

*"The returns are not what counts. It is the satisfaction of
doing something the way you want to do it—of putting into
tangible form what you see in your dreams."*

— Walt Disney

MINTING MONEY

MAY 5, 1987 WAS A much-anticipated day at Disneyland. Guests
began lining up at ticket windows as early as 2 a.m., even though the
festivities would not get underway until 9 a.m. Fans weren't waiting for
the opening of a new park, a new land, or even a new attraction. Nor
were they waiting for a celebrity sighting or the arrival of a distinguished
Disney dignitary. So why the big fuss? This was the day Disney Dollars,
a version of Magic Kingdom currency—the newly minted "coin of the
realm"—were arriving at Disneyland for the first time.

From the back of a Brink's armored truck and accompanied by four
Anaheim policemen, Scrooge McDuck (the world's richest duck, worth
an estimated $27 trillion) delivered the first batch of Disney Dollars.
At first glance, a security presence might seem silly, but these were *real*
dollars—$60,000 to be exact. Each Disney dollar was sold for one US
dollar and can still be used in the parks as currency.

Over time, guests could purchase the dollars at Disneyland, Walt
Disney World, and Disney Stores nationwide. The initial print order

was for one million $1 Mickey Mouse bills, but with their inflated popularity, Disney Dollars were eventually available in the following denominations:

$1—Mickey Mouse

$5—Goofy

$10—Minnie Mouse

$50—Mickey Mouse (added on July 17, 2005 to celebrate Disneyland's Fiftieth Birthday)

Disney Dollars were the brainchild of Jack Lindquist. Jack started working at Disneyland in 1955 as the park's first advertising manager. He went on to serve as marketing director for both Disneyland and Walt Disney World and would cap his career by serving as Disneyland President starting in 1990.

In his book, *In Service to the Mouse,* Jack states that the idea for Disney Dollars came to him while reading the financial page of the newspaper one morning and realizing that "Disneyland was big enough to have its own currency. Eleven to twelve million people a year visit the park and twenty-four million a year visit Walt Disney World. That's more than some small countries."

Wow! You know that your dream has *really* come true when you, like Disneyland and Walt Disney World, are minting money—literally and figuratively!

FUNNY MONEY

NO SUBJECT IS MORE SENSITIVE, including religion or politics, than money. That makes sense because religion and politics *always* involve money. Regardless of your sensitivities and *cents*ibilities (Yes, I just *coined* that word) around money, if you want to get serious about your dream, then you will also need to get serious about your finances.

People are funny when it comes to money. In fact, we are so funny about money that we will even argue over who should and should not appear on the face of our current currencies. While I was writing this book, a passionate argument broke out on social media about whether Harriet Tubman, an Underground Railroad leader in the 1850s, should or should not appear on the new $20 bill. The most common knee-jerk reaction was "no" with the argument being that she never served as a US President and, therefore, wasn't eligible. We've never made an exception for anyone else so why should we make one for her?

Really?

Seriously?

The last time I checked, Benjamin Franklin was never elected President of the United States. And yet somehow my "Benjamins," i.e., $100 bills, work fine in every state in the union. Furthermore, I once won a steak dinner from a colleague who referenced Alexander Hamilton as a former US President during a university commencement speech. When I tried to correct him, kindly of course, before the next ceremony and speech, he argued that Hamilton had to have been President or otherwise there is no way he could appear on the $10 bill.

Ummmmm.

No.

Not so much.

Alexander Hamilton admirably served under our first president, George Washington, as our first treasurer. He never served as president, however, and wasn't even constitutionally eligible to be president because he was born in the British West Indies and, thus, not a natural-born citizen.

I like my steaks medium rare…thank you very much!

But when it comes to money, our emotions are raw.

Very raw.

Walt Disney was the visionary and creative force in the Disney organization, which left Roy with the responsibility for keeping the financial house in order. In an interview for *The American Magazine* in August 1955, just one month after Disneyland opened, Roy had this to say about his younger brother and Walt's funny relationship with the reality of money, "Money is something Walt understands only vaguely, and thinks about only when he doesn't have enough to finance his current enthusiasm, whatever it may be."

Walt often displayed disdain for the almighty dollar. He cared far more about making his dreams come true than he did about making money. Nonetheless, Walt wasn't all fantasy when it came to finances. He recognized the reality of resources and that money, or the lack thereof, was what often stood between him and his next dream. "To tell the truth, (money is) the last thing I think about. The only thing I know is that I have to make dough in order to do things. And my fun has never been in having money. I think I've been the most broke guy in Hollywood."

DO THE MATH

GRANT CARDONE, AN ENTREPRENEURIAL AUTHOR who has gone from drug addict to multi-millionaire, takes a counter-culture approach to money. Like many parents, Grant's mother always told him, "Never talk about money." In contrast, Cardone encourages his readers to talk about money and warns us to avoid those who don't. He writes:

Most people are taught not to talk about money, so it's no wonder they don't have any or have just enough to constantly fret about it. I will never apologize for wanting to get my financials stable, secure, and indestructible.... I will never apologize for wanting money—and I am going to talk about it.

*"What's the use of having eleven octillion dollars
if I don't make a big noise about it?"*

— Scrooge McDuck

So yes, in this chapter we are going to talk about money. But I need to be brutally honest here. I feel somewhat sheepish giving anyone any kind of advice related to numbers, math, or money. I am, after all, a religion major, and religion majors don't do math. There is a reason why the same numbers—3, 7, 10, 12, and 40, keep repeating themselves in the Bible—it makes the math easier—especially for those of us who know we can't do it!

In the interest of full disclosure, I am going to share with you a couple of stories that illustrate the challenges I have faced over the years. First, there was the time Niki and I were visiting my dad in Waverly, Tennessee. We spent the Fourth of July that summer in Florida, and then we drove up to Tennessee the following day. After an all-day drive, Niki and I were starved as we finally pulled into Dad's driveway. As we hugged my dad, I asked, "Do you have any plans for dinner, we are starving!" He said, "I know today is July 5, but Waverly is celebrating the Fourth today. Now, we haven't missed this event in nineteen years, but we can do *whatever* you and Niki want to do."

Nineteen years?

Whatever you and Niki want to do?

Yeah, right.

And oh, by the way, you know you are spending the night in a small town when it takes an extra twenty-four hours for the Fourth of July to arrive.

The next thing Niki and I knew, we were heading straight to Waverly's Fifth of July celebration. Starved, the first booth we found belonged to local firefighters who were raising money by selling a southern summer staple—BBQ. I *love* BBQ and immediately inquired about pricing.

A BBQ sandwich was only three dollars.

A side of coleslaw was only one dollar.

Better yet, you could purchase a combo plate for a full five dollars.

Knowing how hungry I was, I ordered the combo plate, handed over my hard-earned five dollars, and was summarily served a plate that included a single three-dollar sandwich and a one-dollar slaw. I backed away from the booth, scratching my head as I tried to figure out what had just happened.

Niki soon found me, along with the quizzical look on my face. "What's wrong?" she asked.

"Baby, I know we aren't in California anymore, but exactly how backwards can these people possibly be?"

"Why?"

"Well, they are selling BBQ sandwiches for three dollars and a side of slaw for one dollar. But you can get both, via this *combo plate*, for only five dollars! How stupid can they be?" I wanted to know.

Niki wisely responded, "I don't know, dear. Maybe not nearly as stupid as *you* might think. After all, they now have *your* extra dollar!"

On another occasion, I was with a group of friends and we were buying baseball tickets to a sold-out Spring Training game from an "unauthorized" reseller minutes before first pitch. Face value on the ticket was ten dollars, so I made it clear to the scalper that I wasn't willing to pay a penny over face value. "Fine," he responded. "Give me a twenty and I'll give you a five and four ones back."

Thinking that I was only paying nine dollars for a ten-dollar ticket (a five and four ones), I immediately declared, "Deal!" It took my friends several innings to convince me that I had actually paid eleven dollars for the ticket, one dollar *over* face value rather than one under as I had originally thought.

Then there was the time I left an envelope filled with $5,000 in cash sitting at an ATM machine....

These stories are just a few of the reasons why I am admittedly *borrowing* more material from others for this chapter than any other. But no worries, I will be sure to give *credit* to the various contributors!

THE BOTTOM LINE

I DON'T BELIEVE IT IS money that keeps us from our dreams. If this were true, none of us ever would have heard the name "Walt Disney."

Remember, he was bankrupt at age twenty-one—homeless and eating beans out of a garbage can in Kansas City. When it came to his dreams, be it an animation studio, *Steamboat Willie, Snow White and the Seven Dwarfs*, Disneyland, or EPCOT, Walt *never* had enough money.

No, it is our mindset *about* money that keeps us from our dreams. Our current finances may not be enough to fuel our dreams, but they are always more than enough to feed our fears. It is much easier to spend a few dollars on the things that will never matter than it is to take ourselves and our dreams seriously enough to save and sacrifice at a level that might make a real difference one day.

Walt always found a way.

And you can too.

Beyond sacrifice, you might also need to go out on a ledge and go in debt for your dream. Before you gasp, remember we are talking about mindset here. When it comes to mindset and money, I am always amazed by the people more than willing to go in debt for the sake of going to college and/or buying a house, debt that costs hundreds of thousands of dollars, than to go in debt for their dreams. Walt Disney *never* went to college and he *sold* a house to finance his dream of Disneyland. In her book *You Are a Badass*, author Jen Sincero writes about it this way:

> To transform your life, you may have to spend the money you don't have, get a loan, sell something, borrow from a friend, put it on your credit card, or manifest it in some other way. Which is going to go against some pretty deep-seated beliefs we've all been raised with about how going into debt is irresponsible (unless it's a student loan, of course, because for some reason we've decided in that case, and that case only, it's okay). This is about taking a leap of faith into a new realm *that you strongly desire to be in*, demanding of yourself that you rise to the occasion and start living your damn life already.

The bottom line is that our five-dollar coffees and fifty-nine-dollar video games are distractions from the daily grind and an escape from our meaningless jobs that only allow us to make enough money to survive but never really thrive. Too many of us are okay with this because excuses are cheap—cheaper than what it would cost us to find out whether our dream really could make it out of our head and into the marketplace.

> "The three most harmful addictions are heroin, carbohydrates, and a monthly salary."
>
> — Nassim Nicholas Taleb

TAKING STOCK

WITH DISNEYLAND'S ALMOST INSTANT AND overnight success, it is easy to forget the financial risks faced by Walt in seeing his dream of Disneyland come to fruition. Since 1940, Walt Disney Productions had been a publically traded company, so Walt faced serious and significant opposition from stockholders who were only ever beholden to the bottom line. In fact, the opposition to Walt's dream for an amusement park was so intense that, at one point, a select group of stockholders filed a lawsuit to prevent Disneyland from ever becoming a reality. As shared by Disney historian Jim Korkis in *The Unofficial Disneyland 1955 Companion: The Anecdotal Story of the Birth of The Happiest Place on Earth,* Walt addressed the distressed stockholders with this tearful and impassioned speech:

> I don't want this company to stand still. We have prospered before when we have taken chances and tried new things. This is our golden opportunity—a chance to move into an entirely new field. You say we are not in the amusement park

business. No, we're not. But we are in the entertainment business. And amusement parks are entertainment.

I know it is difficult for you to envision Disneyland the way I can. This kind of thing has never been done before. There's nothing like it in the entire world. I know, because I've looked. That's why it can be great, because it will be unique. A new concept in entertainment, and I think…I KNOW…it can be a success!

Today, those same stockholders are known as "The Happiest Stockholders on Earth." Why? Because $1 invested in Disney stock in the 1940s is worth approximately $48,000 dollars today. What a return on investment!

"Dollars are like fertilizer—they make things grow."

— Walt Disney

Speaking of return on investment, just as some people are afraid to spend money on their dreams, others are afraid to make money from their dreams. When you give value, you have every right to expect value in return. Even Walt, who was never interested in making money for the sake of making money, recognized the self-worth that comes from being paid for your dreams as recounted by Jim Korkis in *Walt's Words:*

When I was only eight, I hiked one day down the road to the neighboring farm of Dr. Sherwood, who owned a magnificent chestnut stallion, which was his pride and joy. Perching myself on the spilt-rail fence, I started drawing a sketch of the horse…. [Dr. Sherwood said,] "Don't suppose you'd like to sell that picture?" Dr. Sherwood pressed a coin—a shiny new quarter—carefully into my hand. All the way home, I walked on air, squeezing the quarter so tight it hurt. A wonderful thing had happened! Someone had liked a drawing of mine well enough to buy it. Perhaps now, I would really succeed in my ambition to be a cartoonist!

And succeed he did.

Today, the most frequent complaint I hear about the Disney parks is "Why is it so expensive?" Yet, the second most frequent complaint is "Why is it always so crowded?" What a great business problem to have!

Oh, and the question about why the park(s) are so expensive is not anything new. Walt had to battle this mindset from the very beginning. Compare an interview that Walt gave to Pete Martin of the *Saturday Evening Post* in 1956 with a study in 2016 by Robert Niles of the *Orange County Register*.

The Saturday Evening Post (1956)

Pete Martin: One of the things we should cover is to knock off that rumor that Disneyland's expensive to come to.

Walt Disney: Oh, no. Not at all. That's an old hat thing. You hear it from some people because they don't know what else to say.

By the time this article comes out, I'm raising it to two dollars because I'm adding all these new rides. And to extend my ticket book to take care of the rides, I'm putting this to ten rides for two dollars. Figure it out. It averages twenty cents a ride, doesn't it? It would cost an adult three dollars and a junior two dollars and fifty cents to get in and get ten rides.

If they don't want that, they can pay their buck and pay their fifty cents for their kid and they can come in. They can sit on the park benches, take up the space, dirty up my toilets, litter up the street. They can do all of that if they pay their dollar fifty. They can ride as they want to. They can sit around and hear my band; they can visit my free shows. They can do all that and more for their dollar fifty.

You can't go in a state park without paying that. See, you've got to pay something. You pay so much a head or so much a car to go in a state park. We even have to pay government tax on admission. So it's really ninety-one cents to get in. Now that's what it amounts to. You can't go to the circus for that. I tell you the complaint about the prices is malicious.

Los Angeles is made up of a lot of different characters. How do I know they might not be more interested in some other thing like Marineland? Or some other type of amusement that is competitive. We are competitive, too. Who knows? But there's no foundation for some of these complaints about price. When people make that remark to me, it just sounds to me like they heard it somewhere and they don't know what else to say. How can they compare Disneyland prices with anything else, because there is nothing else like it?

Well, you take your children to Disneyland and for a dollar and a half they get in and spend a whole darn 13 hours if they want to. Now, if you want to go in and buy them expensive toys or you want to buy them bathing suits or your wife happened to go along and sees a wonderful woolen skirt that costs $30, well, people come out and spend all that money. But they don't think twice of going down to Bullocks Wilshire and spending that much on a skirt. If you go into a Broadway department store, you can go in and spend $25 or $30. I'm not insisting people buy things, but I want to give them the opportunity.

The Orange County Register (2016)

Does a ticket to Disneyland cost too much?

I've got to admit that I flinch whenever I look at that $105-a-day cost to visit just one of the Disneyland theme parks on a typical weekend. Yes, I have an annual pass (which I bought—I get no freebies from Disney), but whenever friends or out-of-town guests suggest a Disneyland trip, knowing that I cover theme parks for a living, I brace myself for the blowback when I tell them the price.

But is it too much for what you get? Go online to any Disney fan forum and you won't need too many clicks to find countless fans complaining that Disney's gotten too greedy, that Walt's rolling over in his grave thanks to these prices, and that they'll never buy Disneyland tickets again. Then they do.

Thousands of visitors keep lining up at the gates every day. Whatever Disneyland is charging, it's clearly not too much to keep fans from coming to the park. Granted, many Disneyland fans aren't paying a hundred bucks a day to visit. Many of us have annual passes, and if you use them often enough, the daily cost of a Disneyland trip comes down to less than going to see a movie. But even those infrequent visitors who pay full price for a Disneyland ticket can make an argument that they're paying a fair price for what Disney delivers.

My daughter goes to college in Colorado, and when her friends want to spend the day skiing, they're looking at paying anywhere between $110-$160 for a one-day lift ticket to the popular Vail Resorts. And that's before the cost of buying or renting the skis, boots, snowboard, helmet, goggles or any other gear you need for a day on the trails. Next to that, a $105 Disneyland ticket looks like a bargain.

And don't get me started on golf.

Want to go see the Los Angeles Rams play in their return to Southern California? I found tickets starting at $110 on the NFL's website. That's just for one game—about three to four hours of entertainment—nowhere near the full day you could get at Disneyland.

How about a Broadway show? Fans of the old "Aladdin" show at Disney California Adventure might long to see Disney's longer Broadway version of that production. Get ready to spend between $102 and $274 for a ticket, according to what I found on a popular Broadway ticketing website.

Or you could spend a few bucks less and go see "Aladdin's" replacement at DCA—the new musical "Frozen—Live at the Hyperion"—then spend the rest of the day visiting Cars Land, riding the new Soarin', going on California Screamin' and Tower of Terror, playing Toy Story Midway Mania and drawing pictures at the Animation Academy...instead of fighting with thousands of other theater fans to get a cab or Uber after the show in midtown Manhattan, which seems to be the top post-show pastime on Broadway.

I don't want to apologize for Disney. Heck, I think that skiing, pro sports and Broadway all cost way too much for the average family to enjoy these days, too. But all those other crazy prices show that this isn't just a problem with Disney. It's a bigger problem throughout the live entertainment business.

But the real benefit to rising daily ticket prices for theme parks is how they help upsell visitors to multiday tickets and annual passes. Can't afford to go to Disney for one day? Then come for three days, or five, or 20! It sounds silly when you put it that way, but if parks can get you thinking about the cost *per day*, instead of the total ticket or annual pass price, they can make those passes look like a good deal.

And if making that commitment to visit Disneyland—or other theme parks—again and again and again leaves you with less money for skiing, golf, concerts, theater or games...well, that's not the theme parks' problem.

SOUVENIR STOP

MONEY MINDSET—WE SPENT A GOOD deal of this chapter talking about money and mindset. Write down the first five things that come to your mind when you think about money?

1. _____
2. _____
3. _____
4. _____
5. _____

Review your list and explore these questions. Do you find your list full of hope and imagination or fear and failure? How have your beliefs about money been impacted by your parents, the people you grew up around, and the people you surround yourself with now? What scares you more—spending or making money?

> *"Well, we had a lot of problems putting this thing together.*
> *There was pressure for money. A lot of people didn't*
> *believe in what we were doing."*
>
> — Walt Disney on Disneyland

AUDIT YOUR STORY—WALT DISNEY MOST wanted to be remembered as a storyteller. He built the parks to tell stories. In *The Wisdom of Walt*, I talked about the significance of story and the challenge to live your own great story by constantly editing your activities.

In his book, *A Million Miles in a Thousand Years*, Donald Miller takes story a step further. After purchasing a Roomba vacuum cleaner, for no apparent reason than he had nothing more interesting to do that day, he began to audit his accounts and analyze his ambitions. "I began to realize the stuff I spent money on indicated the stories I was living.... [T]he stuff I spent money on was, in many ways, the sum of my ambitions. And those ambitions weren't the stuff of good stories."

Audit your own expenses from the past thirty days. Note your findings below:

1. What does your audit say about your story?

_____

_____

_____

_____

2. What does your audit say about your ambitions?

_____

_____

_____

_____

3. What does your audit say about your dream?

_____

_____

_____

_____

4. What expenses can you edit immediately so you can get started on your better story?

_____

_____

_____

_____

*"I'm not interested in money, except for what
I can do with it to advance my work."*

— Walt Disney

FIND THE FIFTY-CENT FIX—WALT DISNEY wasn't afraid to spend money—if it added to the show and the overall guest experience. You should do the same. Note, however, that throwing money at a problem isn't always the answer.

Several years ago, a guest shattered the glass in the Haunted Mansion's ballroom scene at Disneyland. Depending on which version of the story you read, the damage came from either a rock or a bullet. The glass is one single sheet and is necessary for creating the "pepper ghost effect" that makes the scene so special. Replacing it would require removing the roof and bringing in a helicopter to remove the original pane and lower a replacement pane. What a pain!

The cost would have been millions of dollars. Instead, an Imagineer ingeniously disguised the damage by creating a spiderweb and covering the hole with a fifty-cent rubber spider procured from a nearby dollar store. Today, when you are riding past the ballroom scene, you can find said spider to the right of the fourth column. Oh, and for the sake of consistency, the same spider was added to Walt Disney World's Haunted Mansion, too.

Don't be afraid to find simple solutions to costly challenges. Keep it simple, especially at the start when resources are most rare.

"Money often costs too much."

— Ralph Waldo Emerson

PICK A PARTNER—WALT DISNEY MAY have been his own boss, but after his bankruptcy in Kansas City, he never rode solo again. It was his partnership with Roy that made his second studio, *The Disney Brothers Studio*, a success. His dream of Disneyland found early believers at the same studio when employees made individual contributions to Walt's amusement park.

Building the park would have been impossible without the partnership of the various sponsors and lessees located throughout the various lands on opening day. Disney repeated the process again at Walt Disney World, especially with Epcot. The budget for Epcot was somewhere between $400 million and $1.2 billion. Regarding the budget, Vice President of contract administration and purchasing, Howard Roland, says, "Over budget? What budget? There was no budget!"

With costs skyrocketing, the company found a partner halfway around the world to help pay the bills. Disney agreed to lend its license to the Oriental Land Company and Tokyo Disneyland to help pay the extraordinary cost of Epcot—with Epcot opening in 1982 and Tokyo Disneyland opening in 1983.

Who can help you with your dream? Selling some of your idea to a partner is a good test of your ability to sell it, period. Even Walt Disney needed partners and so do you.

> *"I remember decisions that were made, such as to go or not go on the Energy pavilion concept which was extraordinary and was going to cost a fortune…. The thing was, if we lost Exxon, we lost EPCOT. It was that simple…. Card Walker was bringing Walt Disney's dream to life, and he didn't want to risk it not being a dream."*
>
> — Tony Baxter

GETTING YOUR HAND STAMPED

BY DESIGN, THIS HAS BEEN one of the book's longest chapters. After all, if I'm going to write about financing your future, I want to make sure my readers receive their money's worth. But before we leave, let's first return to Disneyland. It's 1955, the year the park opened, and the dream that many believed was destined for bankruptcy in six months or less is celebrating its first Christmas season.

Jack Lindquist, the man who brought us Disney Dollars at the start of the chapter, has just started his Disney career as Disneyland's first advertising manager. In his memoir, *In Service to the Mouse,* Jack shares a story that reminds us of the power of dreams and the responsibility we have for seeing our own dreams come true—not for the sake of making as much money as possible but for the simple sake of making as many people happy as possible.

> On Christmas Eve in 1955, I walked up Main Street in the early evening. And on this night, with the garlands

strung between the lampposts, the wreaths hanging in all the store windows, and the huge Christmas tree in Town Square, the atmosphere drew me in.

Because the park was practically empty on that Christmas Eve night, a family caught my attention, and as the mother, father, their 10-year-old son and younger daughter walked down Main Street, I followed them. They were dressed neatly but not stylish; the father and son wore overalls. The mother wore a cotton dress with a coat. They all held hands. They talked to each other and appeared to be a close-knit family.

When they arrived at the Christmas tree in Town Square, next to The Emporium with the mechanical Santa Claus and dolls in the window, the little girl tugged on her mom's arm and said, "Mom, this really was better than having Santa Claus."

I knew then that Santa wasn't bringing them presents. The parents must have told their children that if they went to Disneyland, Santa couldn't bring presents. Right then, I wanted to take them into The Emporium and let them pick out anything they wanted, but, sadly, I didn't have the authority to do so.

The family came to Disneyland but could not afford to spend a lot of money. So, for this family, their time at the park was probably Christmas. The kids would forego toys, and mom and dad wouldn't receive presents.

To me, this one brief moment proved to be my most meaningful memory at the park because it symbolized what we mean to people: We are not a cure for cancer, we are not going to save the world, but if we can make people happy for a few hours for a day, then we are doing something worthwhile.

"The fellow with money is not always the one who is happy. I know chaps almost starving in garrets who are painting what they want and getting more fun out of life than a lot of millionaires."

— Walt Disney

CULTIVATING A CRAZY CULTURE

*"Here's to the crazy ones, the misfits, the rebels, the
troublemakers, the round pegs in the square holes…
the ones who see things differently. They're not fond of rules.
And they have no respect for the status quo. You can
quote them, disagree with them, glorify or vilify them.
About the only thing you can't do is ignore them because
they change things. They push the human race forward.
And while some may see them as the crazy ones,
we see genius. Because the people who are crazy enough to
think they can change the world, are the ones who do."*

— Steve Jobs
Disney's largest stockholder when he died in 2011

THE FIRST FAMILY

I WASN'T THERE IN THE fifth century when the barbarians stormed
the gates of Rome. The closest I have come to such an event is when
I am waiting with other guests for cast members to open the gates to
the Magic Kingdom. Like the barbarians of old, we all want the same
thing—*let us in!*

At Walt Disney World's Magic Kingdom, an interesting ceremony
takes place. Cast members select a family to enter first, and this "Family

of the Day" then assists with the opening ceremony. This is the Magic Kingdom's way of saying "Good morning" to everyone, and it comes complete with characters, a countdown, fireworks, music, and the Mayor of Main Street. It's a big production that Disney cult fans dream of participating in. How does Disney designate its "Family of the Day"? It's a secret, so no one knows for sure. Online tips include arriving early, being energetic, being enthusiastic, and most importantly, being yourself.

The part I find interesting is where the idea originated. Who would think to let guests waiting to storm the kingdom be the ones to throw open the gates? It wasn't Walt's idea. Nor did it come from Roy. It wasn't even a Disney executive's decision. No, this celebrated ceremony that is now a part of the Disney culture came from an hourly cast member. Crazy?

Not when you remember who Walt was and what he set out to create. Walt Disney never cared for corporate hierarchy or structured, organizational charts. Therefore, on any given day, especially Saturdays, you could come to Disneyland and see Walt standing in line with guests at the Jungle Cruise, engineering the Disneyland Railroad, or serving scoops of ice cream on Main Street. Oh, and guess who always gave guests the biggest scoops? Walt Disney!

Walt Disney wasn't just building a kingdom. He was cultivating a culture. A culture focused on "creating happiness" for every guest who entered Disneyland's gates. Walt didn't create this culture by sending a memo or issuing a mandate. He did it by working alongside cast members serving guests and treating *both* as he wished to be treated.

Everyone was family.

BEE INTENTIONAL

WHETHER YOU ARE BUILDING A business, building a dream, or raising a family, always remember that you are also working on a world. *Your* world. Like the countries inside Epcot's World Showcase, your world will develop a culture that defines others' behaviors and expectations. Be intentional about the culture you create. And if you want to change the world, be intentional about cultivating a crazy culture!

Walt Disney had the greatest impact on American culture of any individual in the twentieth century. His crazy dream for an Experimental Prototype Community of Tomorrow was going to revolutionize life in the twenty-first century. His premature death in 1966 prevented his full vision of EPCOT from ever being realized. You can, however, experience a bit of what Walt wanted for EPCOT by venturing into the park's largest pavilion, The Land. Six acres in size, The Land houses a thirteen-minute boat ride, originally called "Listen to the Land," that takes you through four greenhouses, three different ecological environments, and forty different food crops—including fisheries and the future of farming.

When it opened in 1982, Imagineers were proud of what they had accomplished in The Land pavilion because, according to Marty Sklar, "[M]ost Imagineers believed the experience that most exemplified 'Walt's Epcot concept'—experimental prototype of the future—was (and still is) The Land boat ride." This attraction isn't just about agriculture. It is a tribute to Walt Disney from the people who once worked with him and were inspired by the time he spent with them cultivating his crazy dreams for the future.

And Disney almost didn't build it.

Watching grass grow is boring. Disney executives feared that forcing guests to watch lettuce grow would be even more boring.

How did they make this work as a theme park attraction? By putting Imagineers side-by-side with the scientists and cultivating a culture of cooperation. The Imagineers focused on the fun, the entertainment, the storytelling. The scientists, recruited from the University of Arizona and led by atmospheric physicist Dr. Carl Hodges, were responsible for the agricultural know-how. Marty Sklar explains further:

We charged the University of Arizona group with developing the systems for growing food in The Land pavilion's greenhouse-like structures. To prove the principles, in a controlled environment in Arizona, we had them build and plant a third of the total length of what would ultimately be the Florida boat ride. At the pace the boat would travel, we walked the attraction. We could almost pick the corn, tomatoes, banana squash, pineapples (and lettuce!) as we passed by. It was clear that Listen to the Land would be a winner—it was a thrill just to smell the attraction.

Almost as an afterthought, Carl Hodges asked, "Where do we keep the bees?" I looked at him incredulously. "Carl, those boats that will be riding through the greenhouse— they will be filled with real people. Bees are out."

"Well then," Hodges shot back, "how do we *pollinate* the plants?"

"Look," I replied, "we are storytellers. We're in show business. You are the scientists. *You* tell us how you are going to pollinate the plants!"

Today, when you ride the boats…you will very likely see a scientist member of The Land's team pollinating each plant, individually, *by hand*. It takes about fifteen hours per week to pollinate the dozens of plants growing in the Living Laboratories, and they have been doing this for thirty years.

If you want to know how to cultivate your own crazy culture, then *listen to the land. Bee* intentional! If you are a leader, spend time with your people. If you are a parent, spend time with your children. Every day, pollinate with dreams, goals, purpose, and values. Remember well Walt's words, "Sometimes I think of myself as a little bee. I go from one area of the studio to another and gather pollen and sort of stimulate everybody. I guess that's the job I do."

When it comes to culture, just like agriculture, you always reap what you sow. Farmers can't plant radishes in the spring, and then in the fall, think they will be harvesting tomatoes. Likewise, companies can't conduct a "Customer Service Seminar" on Friday afternoon and expect radically different results on Monday morning.

Culture takes time.

It is intentional.

It is who you are.

I once had a ministry student, John, who announced one night that he had inherited some money and was going to use some of it to buy a "Bruce Willis suit." Always curious, I had to know what a "Bruce Willis suit" was.

"Dr. Barnes," he answered, "you know, when you go down to the mall, walk into the finest department store, and tell the salesperson you want their best suit. The one that is so expensive that when you walk out in it, you will look like Bruce Willis."

Looking at John, I replied, "No offense, but there isn't a suit in the world that is going to make *you* look like Bruce Willis."

The following week, the local funeral director was presenting in class. My students were morbidly fascinated with this man's job and the details of body preparation. Trying to lighten things up, and remembering the previous week's suit discussion, I asked the mortician if, with all his makeup artistry, it would be possible to make John look like Bruce Willis.

"Absolutely!" he replied.

Stunned by his response, I slowly stammered out, "How?"

"Easy," was his reply. "Have a closed casket service and put a picture of Bruce Willis on top."

Exactly. Know who you are. Be who you are. Be intentional about cultivating a culture that reflects your worldview, your values, your purpose, and your why. You are dead if you allow anything less.

BREAKING THE RULES

ORGANIZATIONS TAKE ON THE PERSONALITY of their leader. In my world, the world of higher education, this translates into "The campus takes on the personality of the dean." Over the past twenty years, I have had the privilege of playing the part of dean in three different locations. Regardless of where I serve, I always start out with only two rules:

1. Do the right thing.
2. If you can't do the right thing, then don't embarrass the university.

That's it.

We always want to make it more complicated. It's not. This is leadership, not management. This is being a leader, not being a boss. Leave managing to the HR folks, the attorneys, and those interested in serving the status quo.

When I left my first campus in Arizona, after nine years of leadership, my successor was told that he was "inheriting the campus with the most unique culture anywhere in the university system." High praise and a testament to the fact that we often operated as an island of misfits and followed our own, local rules. The culture was intentional because I knew our campus only existed to serve students—students who needed our help to realize their dreams of graduating.

Soon after transferring to Hawaii, a team member came to me early one morning to complain that another staff member was violating the campus dress code. Dress code? I didn't even know our campus had a dress code! The team member presented me with a five-page, front and back, single-spaced document that outlined what you could and could not wear to work. The violation was clear—the offending member was wearing a spaghetti strap dress. Oh no!

I took a moment to think about it, reflected on the fact that we were in Hawaii—the culture that created "Casual Fridays" to encourage people to buy Aloha shirts—and then remembered I was leading a campus that had spent the previous decade running an annual deficit of nearly one million dollars. My vision was to get students graduated, the campus moved to Mililani, and the demoralized staff to realize how awesome they were. I couldn't have cared less about a dress code and spaghetti straps. "Aloha," also means "goodbye," so I shredded the dress code and reminded the reporting team member of my two rules: Do the right thing and don't embarrass the university.

Before you write a rule book, worry first about cultivating a crazy culture. Care about your people and your customers more than you care about your policies and your procedures. Focus on whom you wish to serve and what you want to accomplish.

Most everything else will take care of itself.

> *"If no one ever broke the rules, then we'd never advance.*
> *Leaders must know the rules so that they know when*
> *they should break them and achieve the outcome that*
> *the whole group is deeply committed to."*
>
> — Simon Sinek

NEVER HAD A BOSS LIKE ME!

STATISTICS SHOW THAT 75 PERCENT of people who voluntarily quit their jobs do so because of their bosses, not because of the position. This has certainly been true for me a time or two. In fact, part of the reason why I created *The Wisdom of Walt* as a business is because I wanted the opportunity to work for a boss like me. It sounds egotistical, and maybe it is. But was it egotistical for Walt to treat people the way *he* wanted to be treated?

More than money, people are looking for purpose. Hire based on who believes what you believe, motivate them with vision, and then watch them take you to heights you never believed possible. Along the way, make sure everyone knows why they do what they do and that each person and each task are of equal value. In his book, *Creating Magic,* Lee Cockerell writes about it this way:

> The people who clean the bathrooms, sweep the floors, and empty the garbage are just as important as the executives, managers, directors, and supervisors. Maybe even *more* important. Ditto the ticket takers, the parking lot attendants, and the people who answer the phones. Imagine how many of the Guests at Disney World might vacation someplace else if the bathrooms and floors were dirty or if the people responsible for creating a Guest's first impressions were rude or unhelpful. *Everyone* is important. And this is not just true of theme parks and resorts; it is true of every organization everywhere, including yours.

What Cockerell is conveying is a value that is part of the Disney culture. A culture that was carefully and intentionally cultivated by Walt. In *How to Be Like Walt,* Williams and Denney share a scene from the Disney studio, witnessed by actor Dean Jones, that illustrates the importance of treating everyone equally:

> A gardener at the Disney studio left some tools in an empty parking space. When a producer drove up and saw the tools in his space, he honked at the gardener and gave the poor man a chewing-out. Walt walked up and interrupted the producer's tirade. "Hold it!" he said. "Don't you ever treat one of my employees like that! This man has been

with me longer than you have, so you'd better be good
to him!"

Williams and Denney go on to say, "That was Walt. To his employees,
he was not only a leader. He was their defender and their servant. That's
what separates leaders from bosses."

Lastly, when the going gets rough (and it inevitably will), protect and
defend your people at all cost. How do you create engaged employees,
loyal followers, and customers who are fanatical fans? You can find
answers by reading the story about Roy Disney below. This is told by
Carl Bongirno, former vice president of finance and Walt Disney World
treasurer, in a collection of interviews found in *Walt's People—Volume
11* edited by Didier Ghez :

Once I had an 8 a.m. meeting with Roy. I got there about
7:30 a.m. And I was seated in the outer office with his
administrative assistant Madeleine [Wheeler] who had
been with him for years and years. Madeleine says, "Carl,
excuse me, I have got to get through this tab run before
Roy gets here." She is flipping pages and looking at data
and she has a red marker in her hand and she circles certain
information. She does this for about ten or fifteen minutes
and she gets to the end of the tab listing. She stands up
from her desk and takes it into Roy's office and lays it on
the desk. She comes back out and sits down and says,
"I'm sorry, I just have to have that on Roy's desk every
morning. It is the first thing he does." I said, "Oh, those are
the financial results from yesterday?" She says, "Oh, no,
no, no. Those are the insurance claims from employees.
He wants to see what employees have problems so he can
talk to their managers or supervisors to find out if there
is anything we can do for them." That was top priority for
Roy Disney. Not the financial condition of the company or

what we had done in attendance yesterday at Disneyland. He was looking at the welfare of the employees. That is what the guy did. That is why we had such dedicated, happy, caring workaholics in the company....

SOUVENIR STOP

THE APPLE DOESN'T FALL FAR—WHAT kinds of companies and organizations have your loyalty? Why? Reflect on your experiences and the emotions these memories evoke. People are emotional beings and we *always* remember how something, or someone, made us feel. Culture is king because culture is a *feeling* that oozes out of an organization.

One of the worst days of my life was running over my iPhone and iPad on a California freeway. I will always remember Apple replacing my electronics at a significantly discounted rate and making me feel better by the end of that awful evening. The accident was my fault, but that didn't stop Apple from doing a good thing.

> *"Being the richest man in the cemetery doesn't matter to me.... Going to bed at night saying we've done something wonderful...that's what matters to me."*
>
> — Steve Jobs

BLOOM WHERE YOU ARE PLANTED—YOU may not be *the* leader of your organization, but that doesn't mean you can't have a cultural impact in your current position. Start doing the right thing. Don't wait for permission. *Bee* the change you are looking for and trust that over time, and with a little pollination, others will follow.

Use the space below to write down how you wish to be treated as a customer and coworker:

Now, go and do likewise.

Harvest Fun—I make having fun a syllabus requirement in every course I teach. I value having a good time, and I encourage students to do the same.

Having fun is also an office value. Our team plays ping-pong, goes bowling, goes to baseball games, and celebrates major and minor milestones. Set a date below to take your team off-site for the sole purpose of having fun. Where will you go? What will you do? Go crazy and have fun!

_____

_____

GETTING YOUR HAND STAMPED

People often ask whether I have ever worked for Disney. The answer is "no." So how can I possibly know so much about Walt Disney, Disney, and Disneyland? The answer lies in a crazy obsession. An obsession that started by observing my dad.

While I was growing up, my dad was in the Air Force and worked on the side as a manager at a fast-food restaurant. As an enlisted man with four children, having the extra job as a manager was how he paid the bills. I couldn't go with my dad to his military job, but I often accompanied him to his restaurant. I would hide out in the small office behind the kitchen or do homework at a table in the dining room. This was a chance to be with my dad, watch him work, and eat some free hamburgers and French fries.

One afternoon while I was working on homework, a family with young children came in, ordered their food, and sat at a nearby table to enjoy their meal. One of the younger children started goofing off and knocked over an entire tray of drinks. Hearing the commotion, my dad rushed out of the kitchen, mopped up the mess, and replaced all the drinks. No questions asked.

Mystified, I started asking my dad questions. "Why were you so quick to replace all of those drinks? You didn't even ask what happened? It was that kid's fault and not the restaurant's."

My dad responded with words I have never forgotten. "Son, the cost of those drinks or that meal is pennies. The value of having that family as loyal customers for life is priceless."

Disney does the same, as illustrated in "The $100,000 Salt and Pepper Shaker" by Randy Pausch from *The Last Lecture*. See if this story doesn't sound familiar:

> When I was twelve years old and my sister was fourteen, our family went to Disney World in Orlando. Our parents figured we were just old enough to roam a bit around the park without being monitored. In those days before cell phones, Mom and Dad told us to be careful, picked a spot where we would meet ninety minutes later, and then they let us take off.

> Think of the thrill that was! We were in the coolest place imaginable and we had the freedom to explore it on our own. We were also extremely grateful to our parents for taking us there, and for recognizing we were mature enough to be by ourselves. So, we decided to thank them by pooling our allowances and getting them a present.

> We went into a store and found what we considered the perfect gift: a ceramic salt and pepper shaker featuring two bears hanging off a tree, each one holding a shaker. We paid ten dollars for the gift, headed out of the store, and skipped up Main Street in search of the next attraction.

> I was holding the gift, and in a horrible instant, it slipped out of my hands. The thing broke on impact. My sister and I were both in tears.

An adult guest in the park saw what happened and came over to us. "Take it back to the store," she suggested. "I'm sure they'll give you a new one."

"I can't do that," I said. "It was my fault. I dropped it. Why would the store give us another one?"

"Try anyway," the adult said. "You never know."

So we went back to the store—and we didn't lie. We explained what happened. The employees in the store listened to our sad story, smiled at us—and told us we could have a new salt and pepper shaker. They even said it was their fault because they hadn't wrapped the original salt and pepper shaker well enough! Their message was "Our packaging should have been able to withstand a fall due to a twelve-year-old's overexcitement!"

I was in shock. Not just gratitude, but disbelief. My sister and I left the store completely giddy.

When my parents learned of the incident, it really increased their appreciation of Disney World. In fact, that one customer-service decision over a ten-dollar salt and pepper shaker would end up earning Disney more than $100,000.

Let me explain.

Years later, as a Disney Imagineering consultant, I would sometimes end up chatting with executives pretty high up in the Disney chain of command, and wherever I could I would tell them the story of the salt and pepper shaker.

I would explain how the people in that gift shop made my sister and me feel so good about Disney, and how that led my parents to appreciate the institution on a whole other level.

My parents made visits to Disney World an integral part of their volunteer work. They had a twenty-two-passenger bus they would use to drive English-as-a-second-language students from Maryland down to see the park. For more than twenty years, my dad bought tickets for dozens of kids to go to Disney World. I went on most of those trips.

All in all, since that day, my family has spent more than $100,000 at Disney World on tickets, food and souvenirs for ourselves and others.

Is it crazy to think that a $10 salt and pepper shaker can result in $100,000 in revenue? Yes! But it begins to make sense when you remember that Walt was crazy enough to shake things up in the hospitality and service industry by doing everything dramatically different in Disneyland. He hired cast members committed to creating happiness and cultivated them by showing them how. You, too, can cultivate a crazy culture by giving your staff, your team, your kids something worth watching.

Thanks, Dad.

> *"Who you are is who you attract. If you want to attract better people, become the kind of person you desire to attract."*
>
> — John Maxwell

COMMUNICATING CLEARLY

"We are alone, struggling to survive until we learn to communicate with one another."

— Dame Judi Dench
Narrator, Spaceship Earth

WRITING ON THE WALL

EPCOT WAS DISNEY'S FIRST ATTEMPT at a "non-castle" park. Nonetheless, Epcot, like every Disney park, needed some sort of centerpiece—an iconic symbol that could communicate to every guest where they were and, more importantly, *why* they were there. For Epcot, that symbol would be Spaceship Earth.

Inspired by the famed futurist R. Buckminster Fuller, who wrote a short book entitled *Operating Manual for Spaceship Earth* in 1968, Imagineers engineered Epcot's Spaceship Earth—the world's first, and largest, geodesic sphere. It is eighteen stories high, 165 feet wide, sits on three pairs of legs, weighs sixteen million pounds and took twenty-six months to build. Because it stands in the center of Future World and in front of World Showcase, it is Spaceship Earth that says, "Hello" as you enter Epcot and "Goodbye" as you exit—a message that is not easily forgotten.

178 BEYOND THE WISDOM OF WALT

I first visited Epcot in 2013, thirty-one years after it opened. For three decades, I had seen the pictures and postcards of Spaceship Earth and dismissed it as an oversized golf ball. I am not alone. Guests frequently refer to Epcot's logo and focal point, Spaceship Earth, as "that golf ball thing." But it is so much more.

Spaceship Earth is home to a headliner attraction that tells the history of human communication. Riding in Omnimover vehicles, guests spiral through serpentine scenes that travel through time starting with cavemen communicating with paintings and ending with today's home computers and a cupola view of Earth surrounded by a star-studded planetarium. Highlights include the Egyptians using hieroglyphics, the Phoenicians employing an alphabet, the fall of Rome, including the preservation of ancient texts by Jewish and Islamic scholars, and the introduction of the Information Age with the invention of the moveable type printing press by Johannes Gutenberg. What goes up must come down, so guests rotate 180 degrees and ride backwards for the long descent from the top of Spaceship Earth to the unloading area below. The attraction includes twenty Audio-Animatronics scenes, and the backstage area is so complex that, according to Alex Wright in *The Imagineering Field Guide to Epcot at Walt Disney World,* "maintenance workers occasionally resort to drawing pencil lines on the walls (like bread crumbs) to find their way back where they started."

For Niki and me, Spaceship Earth is a favorite attraction at Walt Disney World and a must-do attraction every time we visit Epcot. Yes, it is educational. But it is education communicated in a compelling way. It reminds us that communicating clearly is an essential life skill and that your success, like the success of all mankind, is contingent on communication.

I have a lot to say in this chapter. But one of the keys to communicating clearly is keeping things short and simple. Therefore, I don't want this chapter to take longer to read than it does for you to ride Spaceship Earth—fifteen minutes. Disney's Omnimovers not only allow for maximum capacity, 2,400 guests per hour for Spaceship Earth, but they also guide your experience by forcing you to focus only on what the show directors want you to see. As I move you through this chapter, we will focus on the importance of casting a compelling vision, speaking truthfully, and asking questions. Ready to board?

TUNNEL VISION

WALT DISNEY MOST WANTED TO be remembered as a storyteller, and he built Disneyland to tell stories. People in Hollywood who worked with Walt remember him as "the best storyteller in the business." What made Walt such a good storyteller and thus a compelling communicator? He was willing to cut anything that did not move the story forward. Examples of this exist in both his cartoons, full-length animated feature-films, and his live-action movies. But I want to share an example from Disneyland. When guests walk into the Magic Kingdom, it is as if they are stepping through the movie screen and into the story. Therefore, there are tunnels on each side of the entrance, stage left and stage right, with Walt's vision statement hanging overhead:

"Here you leave today and enter the world of yesterday, tomorrow and fantasy."

Every Disney fan who frequents the Magic Kingdom has seen these words, and you may even have them memorized. Here is what you may not know. When Disneyland opened on July 17, 1955, the plaques weren't there. Not because of a construction delay but because Walt was still working on the wording. Memos exist, in Walt's own handwriting, that show the original text saying: *"**Where** you leave today and **visit** the world of yesterday, tomorrow and fantasy."* It is only a two-word difference, but those two words make all the difference. These thirteen words are Walt's vision statement for Disneyland. Walt knew the importance of vision, so he was willing to wait an extra two weeks to make sure his vision statement was short, sweet, and just right.

Everyone, corporations and individuals alike, needs a vision statement. Why do you exist? Why do you do what you do? Where are you? Where do you want to be? Why do you want to get there?

Chances are you either don't have a vision statement, or the one you do have stinks. How do I know? Because every day I walk into offices with walls filled with vision statements, mission statements, and a long list of "core values." They make for nice decorations, but unless you, and every other employee, can recite these statements verbatim, live and breathe by these values, and are willing to die for these declarations, they are worthless.

Keep it short and simple. Walt didn't need more than thirteen words to cast his vision for Disneyland. Neither do you. Oh, and in case you are curious, as Dean of Student Success, the vision for me and my team is *"From the Classroom to Commencement"*—a reflection of our desire to see students graduate.

> *"Effective leaders don't have to be passionate. They don't have to be charming. They don't have to be brilliant. They don't have to possess the common touch. They don't have to be great speakers. What they must be is clear."*
>
> — Marcus Buckingham and Curt Coffman

I AM GROOT

WHEN IT COMES TO SIMPLE communication, I don't believe it gets any simpler than the character Groot from the Guardians of the Galaxy movie franchise. Groot is an extraterrestrial, tree-like creature who's only dialogue, ever, is "I am Groot." It is an ongoing gag throughout the movies, and because of his origins as a tree root, Groot reminds me not only to speak simply but also truthfully.

Why truthfully?

I have a colleague, Michael, who recently moved from an apartment to a house. He was excited about the house because it offered both a larger living space and a lawn. Michael was looking forward to having property he could personally care for, and he couldn't wait to acquire his first man tools—a lawnmower, leaf blower, weed whacker, rake, pruning shears, gardening gloves, and watering can.

You get the picture.

Michael returned to work after his first weekend of yard work, devastated, because he broke his brand-new lawnmower by "running over a tree stump." He didn't get to work on his lawn, *and* he was out hundreds of dollars in repair costs.

Twenty-four hours later, we learned the real story. Yes, he had broken his lawnmower, but it wasn't from running over a tree stump. The truth was he had run over a can of whipped cream.

Why the lie?

Mr. Michael didn't want to risk his man card, so he told the tree stump story instead—a harmless lie, but one that we give him endless grief for to this day.

I am always up for a good story. Like Mark Twain and Walt Disney, I never let "facts get in the way of a good story." There are times, however, when we must step out of story/spin mode and speak truthfully. In his book, *Creating Magic: 10 Common Sense Leadership Strategies from a Life at Disney,* Lee Cockerell says that our ability to lead is rooted in our ability to communicate clearly, directly, and honestly:

> Good communication is *clear* communication. Use ordinary language, and say exactly what you mean. If you don't, people will leave more confused than they were before, and you'll pay the price in inefficiency and loss of trust. Beating around the bush increases confusion, not clarity. If you "spin" your message, people will see right through it, and their trust in you will be undermined, perhaps forever. If you communicate directly, and honestly,

all the time, people will understand what you want them to know and what you want them to do. And you will earn a reputation as a trustworthy individual. People may not always like what you say, but at least they will trust that you mean it. Nothing is more important if you want to be a great leader.

I grew up in a family where it wasn't okay to speak the truth. Naturally, this has created a lot of dysfunction over the years. This was never clearer to me than a few years ago when I was home in Florida and enjoying a summer evening with my young nieces and nephews around the common area pool at my mom's condominium complex. One of the younger kids had an "accident" in the pool. For a few minutes, everyone wanted to pretend that nothing had happened and ignore the obvious poop floating on the top. This became impossible when the oldest child took notice, broke the silence, and started screaming, "There's poop in the pool! There's poop in the pool!"

The truth-telling "whistle blower" was pulled promptly from the pool before the poop was and severely disciplined. Why? He had broken Unspoken Family Rule #1: *Never speak an uncomfortable truth and NEVER speak an uncomfortable truth in public!*

Today, I have more than my fair share of dysfunctions. Fortunately, an unwillingness to speak the truth isn't one of them. In high school, I was voted "most likely to say something," and today, my family, friends, and students swear that I missed my calling as Simon Cowell, the truth-telling judge on *American Idol*. So, if you lie to me about how you broke your lawn mower, then I am going to call you out and cut you deep.

How clean is your pool?

Niki is no different. I shared in *The Wisdom of Walt* that we, like Walt and Lilly, met while working together. Early on, Niki encountered me as "the boss" and told me a truth I didn't want to hear but certainly needed to know.

The university we worked for had mailed a diploma without packing it properly. This priceless document arrived folded, spindled, and mutilated. I was mortified and immediately picked up the phone to call our Registrar's Office. The poor soul who took the call on the other end received an earful of righteous indignation.

Unbeknownst to me, Niki, our newest team member, was standing in my doorway. She had arrived to pick up the mail, overheard the screaming, and explored further. The second I slammed down the phone, she stepped into my office, looked me in the eye, and spoke truth: "I know I'm new here. I have no idea who you were talking to or what any of this was even about. What I do know is that as long as I work here, I don't *ever* want to hear you talk to another human being like that again."

Wow! Forget love at first sight. This was love at first fight! But Niki was right. Niki is always right. I had every right to be upset about the situation, but as the leader, it was my responsibility to set the tone. How we speak is as important as what we say—a truth Niki never hesitates to remind me of.

Even now.

> *"A person's success in life can usually be measured*
> *by the number of uncomfortable conversations*
> *he or she is willing to have."*
>
> — Tim Ferriss

YOU HAVE NOT, BECAUSE YOU ASK NOT

LASTLY, I WANT TO FOCUS on the importance of asking. Albert Einstein once claimed that, "I have no special talent. I am only passionately curious." Another similar statement, by bestselling author Alex Lightman, says that, "The quality of your life is directly related to the quality, quantity, and variety of your questions." When you aren't getting the results you want, it's time to get insatiably curious and start asking better questions.

If you lead, manage, or supervise people, I want to encourage you to listen to Brian Grazer. Who is Brian Grazer? I'm glad you asked!

Brian Grazer is a Hollywood producer whose movies, to date, have generated more than $13 billion in box office revenues. He has collected 43 Academy Awards and 131 Emmy nominations. His movie, *A Beautiful Mind,* won "Best Picture" in 2002. His first film nomination came more than thirty years ago when he produced the 1984 movie *Splash*—the first Disney movie under their new Touchstone label, one of the first PG-rated Disney movies, and the film that inspired the name for Disney's popular attraction Splash Mountain. (Before *Splash*, the plan was to name the log flume ride "Zip-A-Dee-Doo-Dah River Run.")

In 2015, Brian Grazer made another splash when he wrote his first book, *A Curious Mind: The Secret to a Bigger Life.* One of the gems in this best-seller is to stop bossing people around by telling them what to do. Instead, manage with curiosity and start asking questions. Grazer goes further and writes:

Sometimes you have to give orders.

Sometimes I have to give orders.

But if you set aside the routine instructions that are part of everyone's workday—the request to get someone on the phone, to look up a fact, to schedule a meeting—I almost always start with questions.

I especially think questions are a great management tool when I think someone isn't doing what I would hope they would, or when I think something isn't going in the direction I want it to go.

People often imagine that if there's going to be conflict, they need to start with a firm hand, they need to remind people of the chain of command.

I'm never worried about who is in charge.

I'm worried about making sure we get the best possible decision, the best possible casting, script, movie trailer, financing deal, the best possible movie.

Asking questions elicits information, of course.

Asking questions creates the space for people to raise issues they are worried about that the boss, or their colleagues, may not know about.

Asking questions gives people the chance to tell a different story than the one you're expecting.

Most important from my perspective is asking questions means people have to make their case for the way they want a decision to go.

If you are a dreamer, an entrepreneur, or an individual committed to success, then it is even more imperative that you get good at asking— asking questions, asking for help, asking for anything.

Our daughter, Bethany, reminded me a few years ago that many of us are often reluctant to ask. During Bethany's first year living in Las Vegas, Niki and I visited her over the Thanksgiving weekend. Excited about her new city, Bethany insisted on taking us out on the town and showing us her favorite Vegas venues. That first night, we crisscrossed the Strip like Walt Disney World Park Hoppers—complete with monorail.

Near midnight, and with me already well beyond bedtime, we found ourselves deep inside Caesar's Palace. Bethany was looking for Gordon Ramsay's Pub, a place she had heard about but had never actually visited. All roads might lead to Rome, but it soon became obvious that we were never going to find this pub without first stopping for directions. I begged Bethany to ask, but she refused, convinced that Gordon Ramsay's was "just around the river bend."

Frustrated, I just stopped. "I'm not taking another step until you ask someone for help," I declared. "After all, you are an award-winning, investigative journalist. You make your living asking people questions!"

Bethany countered with, "I'm on vacation! If you want to ask someone, fine. But I'm not doing it!"

I took off, asked an employee for help, and returned.

"Well?" Bethany asked.

"Well, what?" I responded.

"Well, did you get the directions?"

"Yup," I replied.

"Well, are you going to tell us?" Bethany wanted to know.

"No," I replied.

"Why not?" Bethany asked.

"Because I am an educator. And I'm on vacation!"

In Bethany's defense, maybe she didn't want to come off like a guest on vacation at Walt Disney World. On any given day, the 66,000 plus cast members are asked a series of obvious and/or silly questions. Examples, courtesy of David Koenig, in *Realityland*, include:

What time is the 3:00 parade?
Are you part of the scenery or do you work here?
This place cost over 400 million? Do you have any idea what that is in dollars and cents?
Is this bus going to the Polyester Hotel?
Where is Harry Potter Land?
Is that the Fairy Godfather's Castle?

Is this the way to Fancy Land?

Can you show me the way to Toilet Land?

When it comes to success, there is no such thing as an obvious or silly question. You can't know everything, and you certainly can't do everything. The solution? Ask!

Readers often ask me questions about *The Wisdom of Walt*. One of the most frequent questions, especially from folks in Southern California, relates to the foreword written by Garner Holt and Bill Butler of Garner Holt Productions. Locals recognize the name and know that Garner Holt Productions is the world's largest maker of Audio-Animatronics, including the cars in Radiator Springs Racers and the fantastic, fire-breathing dragon that Mickey slays during Disneyland's Fantasmic.

"Wow! Your foreword was written by Garner Holt" is typically followed up with, "How?" How did you get Garner Holt and Bill Butler of Garner Holt Productions to write your foreword? That is awesome!"

The answer, of course, is: I asked!

How did I get Lee Cockerell to write the foreword for this book? You guessed it! I asked.

Before we exit and head to our Souvenir Stop, I want to ask your indulgence and share one more story. In 1971, Walt Disney World opened as "The Vacation Kingdom of The World." This tagline promoted the idea of a resort that included more than just a theme park. Walt Disney World came complete with hotels, water sports, and even golf. Disney knew how to promote the theme park, but selling the rest of the resort and convincing guests to stay longer than a single day required promoting the other Vacation Kingdom activities. "The Mad Tee Party" by David Koenig is a story about marketing more than the Magic Kingdom and a reminder of the magic that can come from asking:

In addition to trying to convince people to visit an empty park, marketing director Sandy Quinn also was scrambling to throw together a world-class golf tournament. Shortly before the park opened, Card Walker told Quinn to try to organize a PGA golf tournament with the likes of Arnold Palmer and Jack Nicklaus. Quinn knew nothing about golf, but was able to set up an appointment with PGA Tour commissioner Joe Dey. A distinguished older gentleman, Dey was intrigued by the scrappy young man's vision. By the end of the meeting, Walt Disney World had a date on the PGA tour: the week after Thanksgiving. It just didn't have any golfers.

As luck would have it, when Quinn returned to Disney World he heard that Arnold Palmer was just a few miles away, at a new country club he helped build in Bay Hill. Quinn immediately headed for Bay Hill and convinced Palmer to stop by for a tour of Disney's new courses. Quinn began rhapsodizing about the first PGA event where the entire family could enjoy itself, as he and Palmer climbed into a golf cart. But as they motored up and down the gorgeous fairways, Palmer kept staring off into the distance, seemingly oblivious to Quinn's sales pitch. Arnie, a private pilot, was enamored with the monorail.

Quinn drove him to the round house, where engineers were prepared to take a monorail on a test run. "Can I have a ride?" Palmer asked. The workmen consented. Palmer jumped in and rode around the track for hours. As the golf legend finally climbed out of the monorail, Quinn again mentioned the golf tournament idea. "No problem," Palmer said. "Sign me up. I'll call a few friends." Using Palmer's pull, Disney was able to attract a full roster of name golfers—including Leslie Trevino, Billy Casper, Chi Chi Rodriguez, and a first-year winner Nicklaus—and plenty of publicity for Disney World and its inaugural Walt Disney World Classic.

"Life favors the specific ask and punishes the vague wish."

— Tim Ferriss

SOUVENIR STOP

WRITE YOUR VISION STATEMENT—WHAT DOES success look like for you and your business? Use the lines below to cast your vision. Remember to communicate clearly and limit yourself to no more than thirteen words. Thirteen was Walt Disney's favorite number, thus the official address for Disneyland is 1313 Harbor Boulevard, *and* Walt only needed thirteen words for his vision statement over the tunnel entrances into the Magic Kingdom.

Have fun with this and take your time. When it came to Disneyland, Walt waited until he had it just right!

_____

_____

_____

_____

TRUTH CHALLENGE—WHAT DIFFICULT CONVERSATION HAVE you been putting off? With whom? Why? Commit below to a date and time to have this talk and write down the result you wish to achieve. You only have to follow one rule: Be Truthful!

_____

_____

_____

_____

ASK YOURSELF—I HAVE THREE SETS of questions for you:

1. What do you do more often? Give instructions or ask questions? Why?

_____

_____

_____

2. What do you need to know, and whom do you need to ask to help take your team, your dream, and your goal to the next level? Write these questions down and commit to a date and time for asking them.

_____

_____

_____

3. Per Tim Ferriss, look at your to-do list and ask: "Which *one* of these, if done, would render all the rest either easier or completely irrelevant? When will you do that *one* thing?

_____

_____

_____

BONUS SOUVENIR STOP

TWO BUILDINGS RADIATE OUT FROM Spaceship Earth: Innoventions East and Innoventions West. Originally called Communicore East and Communicore West, these buildings are the core of Epcot's Future World and are filled with hands-on exhibits, displays, shops, and restaurants. In honor of each, I offer you the following communication challenges:

WRITTEN WORD—SCOTT ADAMS, CREATOR OF the Dilbert comic strip, wrote a one-page, eight-paragraph piece *The Day You Became a*

Better Writer that will teach you more about writing in five minutes than you will learn in a year-long writing course. Highlights include:

1. Aim for clarity and persuasion.
2. Prune your extra sentences. Don't use two words when one will do.
3. Find funny words.
4. Your first sentences are key. Keep it curious and grab your reader.
5. Write short sentences. Write short sentences. Write short sentences.
6. Write in active voice (subject/verb) vs. passive voice (verb/subject).

FYI: I share this piece with students every semester. You are getting it tuition-free.

Read the full piece at: http://blog.dilbert.com/post/127310496506/the-day-you-became-a-better-writer-2nd-look

UNSPOKEN WORD—WHAT YOU DON'T SAY is as important, maybe more so, than what you do say. For example, Walt Disney seriously considered St. Louis as a site for an East Coast Disneyland. But at a dinner party one night, August (Gussie) Busch, Jr. raised, again, the issue of selling liquor inside the park. Here is what he said to Walt: "Any man who thinks he can design an attraction that is going to be a success in this city and not serve beer or liquor, ought to have his head examined." What did Walt say in response? Nothing. He kept looking and eventually located in Orlando. Today, many historians believe Busch's comments cost St. Louis the opportunity to be home to Walt Disney World.

> *"Listen has the same letters as silent. The average human says 10,000 words a day. Maybe cut that in half. When you listen, you add. When you talk, you subtract."*
>
> — James Altucher

GETTING YOUR HAND STAMPED

DISNEYLAND WAS ALWAYS GOING TO have a castle. The only question was, "What will Walt name it?" During development, and continuing through construction of the park, names for the symbolic structure vacillated from "Medieval Castle," "Fantasyland Castle," and "Fairy Castle" to "Snow White Castle" and "Robin Hood Castle." Walt settled on "Sleeping Beauty Castle," if for no other reason than because *Sleeping Beauty* was the animated feature in production at the Disney Studio in Burbank. Time spent building Disneyland delayed the release of *Sleeping Beauty* (until 1959), but Walt was hoping that the marketing tie-in between the park and film would boost ticket sales to both Disneyland *and* Sleeping Beauty.

Walt Disney World follows the overall design and layout of Disneyland, only on a larger scale. It, too, has a castle sitting center stage—but Orlando's is 189 feet tall versus her older sister, sitting center stage in Anaheim, at 77 feet tall. Both were designed by Disney Legend, Herb Ryman, with Walt Disney World's version being named for Niki's favorite princess, Cinderella—an option originally considered at Disneyland.

The primary purpose of any Disney park icon is to communicate. Yes, Spaceship Earth is the icon that holds an attraction telling the story of human communication, but every park centerpiece—from Sleeping Beauty Castle in Anaheim to Animal Kingdom's Tree of Life in Orlando—sets the tone for its respective park, communicates a story, and helps orient us to our surroundings.

As a storyteller and visionary leader, Walt Disney understood the importance of communication. People often question why Sleeping Beauty Castle, standing at a mere seventy-seven feet, is *so* small. They don't realize that, "Walt Disney recalled the European castles of old were often built to intimidate the peasants. He believed a less-imposing castle would appear friendlier and more inviting to Disneyland guests, and thus Sleeping Beauty Castle is smaller than any other Disney theme park castle."

Whenever anyone complained to Walt that his castle was too small to fit their own fancy, Walt challenged them to get down on their hands and knees and view Disneyland's centerpiece not from their own eyes but from the perspective and eyes of a small child.

Message received.

> *"But the order here at Disneyland works on people,*
> *the sense of harmony. They feel more content here, in a way*
> *that they can't explain. You find strangers talking to*
> *each other without any fear."*
>
> — John Hench

KEEPING IT CLEAN

"Walt Disney...always bent down to pick up stray trash in the parks. Frank [Wells] and I took our cue from Walt."

— Michael Eisner
Chief Executive Officer of the Walt Disney Company,
1984-2005

20,000 LEAKS UNDER THE SEA

I WAS TEN YEARS OLD when I first walked into a Disney Park, Florida's Magic Kingdom, in 1974. At that age, I was still young enough to be mesmerized by the magic but already old enough not to buy into all the illusions. I no longer believed in Santa Claus, so you certainly weren't going to convince me that ghosts had haunted a mansion, that bears could put together a country jamboree, or that pirates were pillaging and plundering a village. These were nice stories, sure. But real? No way.

The submarines, however, had me convinced. Deeply. What boy wouldn't want the chance to go underwater and travel through liquid space? Who could resist Captain Nemo and his call to "Dive! Dive! Dive!"? It wasn't until years later that I learned the hard truth. The submarines weren't *really* submarines and you never *actually* go under water. Imagineers created the diving illusion by sitting guests below the water line and then blowing bubbles past the porthole windows to simulate downward movement. Our own imaginations take over from there.

When I returned to Florida's Magic Kingdom in 2013, my first visit as an adult, I learned another hard truth. My submarines were gone. Long gone. They were closed for refurbishment in 1994 and then officially closed two years later without having ever returned.

What happened to my memories? My childhood?

Two words you never think about when you are a kid but are constant realities in the real world of being an adult: money and maintenance.

Disneyland opened its submarine voyage in 1959 with realistic vessels made of metal. Florida's, however, were crafted from fiberglass that matched the Nautilus design from the 1954 Disney movie that gave the attraction its name. The Victorian, steampunk subs looked great, but they were a nightmare to maintain. They expanded in the heat of the sun and contracted under the cool of the water. Cracks opened, so cast members were constantly patching leaks. By 1994, the cost of closing the leaks and cleaning the 11.5-million-gallon lagoon while maintaining dozens of submerged Audio-Animatronics became too much even for Disney's deep pockets. The subs may have been in Fantasyland, but the realities of the real world sunk them.

You can still go "under the sea" where the subs once sat, only now it is with Ariel and her assortment of friends from *The Little Mermaid*. But it's just not the same. Nonetheless, the story of the subs is a reminder of an important transition we all must make from being a child to being an adult. Keeping stuff clean and maintained matters. It especially matters when you want to be a "part of that world" called Success.

HERE'S TO THE MESS WE MAKE

CHILDREN ARE MESSY.

Dreamers are messier.

I know because I am both. Which is why it is a miracle that my mom and I never killed each other.

Mom first visited Disneyland in 1960, five years after it opened and three years before I was added as the family's newest attraction. She shared stories from her trip to the Magic Kingdom, but none of her tales included anything about a ride, attraction, show, parade, or souvenir. Instead, all she talked about was what she appreciated the most—how clean Disneyland was. I now realize that this one trip—taken during her still formative, young adult years—had a huge influence on her motherly methodologies. Like Walt and Disneyland, my mom was obsessed with cleanliness. During my teenage years, when every parent stands as a target in the Frontierland Shooting Gallery, I griped to my friends that I had the mother who could keep the White House clean. Since then, I have been to both the White House and Disneyland. The White House is certainly clean enough, but I now know that I wasn't totally accurate. My mom could do more—my mom could keep Disneyland clean!

Childhood traumas include being on my hands and knees every morning before school to straighten the tassels on the super-sized shag rug that sat under our dining room table (akin to cast members raking rice out of the sand at the Polynesian Resort at Walt Disney World. Yes, they do that). Another favorite was spending an entire weekend cleaning the house from top to bottom only to have my mom go to the one place no child could reach or would ever even think about cleaning—the top of the refrigerator.

Mom has been dead for nearly a decade (No, I didn't do it), but I can still hear her now. Even as an adult, my inner child fears making a midnight snack because "The kitchen is closed!" When playing a video game, I sometimes shudder thinking, "Toy time is over!" The worst is when I can't find something and her words from another world shout into my ear, "Jeff, how many times do I have to tell you? A place for everything and everything in its place!"

The closest we ever came to blows wasn't when I was a teenager but when I was in my forties. I brought a friend from Arizona, Randy, home with me to Florida for a weekend of scuba diving (a substitute for submarines). Randy is eight years older than me, but that didn't keep my mom from constantly calling him "my little friend." At breakfast one morning, she thanked "my little friend" for making his bed and then turned to me and said, "Jeff, I know the only reason you bothered to make your bed this morning is because your 'little friend' made his and you didn't want your 'little friend' to embarrass you."

Right, mom. Because nothing about any of this wasn't *already* embarrassing.

Yes, growing up, there was conflict between my mom and me over her cleanliness and my messiness. But like every mom, your mom included, my mom was right. Clean counts and maintenance matters. Walt's dream for Disneyland tells us why.

Before Disneyland, Americans associated amusement parks with seaside locations staffed by seedy, seasonal workers. This is why Walt's wife, Lilly, wanted nothing to do with his dream. If she didn't want to go to an amusement park, why would she want to own one? Walt promised her a spotless park, and when he delivered Disneyland with streets so clean guests could eat off the pavement, he raised the expectations for public places across the United States.

Today, keeping everything clean and well-maintained is a core element of Disney's cultural identity. Understanding why Walt set such high standards requires an understanding of American culture in the 1950s. Sam Gennawey explains further in *Walt Disney and the Promise of Progress City:*

> Walt sensed there was a change happening in the American culture. Families in the 1950s had begun to reset their expectations for what was meant by progress. There was a growing national consensus that proclaimed that cleanliness and uniformity was a sign of progress. With the spread of freeways, people preferred to patronize modern, familiar motel chains and eat in clean coffee shops.... Walt assumed correctly that they would want to visit a different

type of family amusement park as well. . . . When Walt gave a tour of the park, a journalist commented that everything would soon be covered in litter. Walt curtly replied, "It'll never happen." "Why not?" asked the reporter. "Because, we're going to make it so clean people are going to be embarrassed to throw anything on the ground." Walt was right. Disneyland had validated people's expectations for cleanliness of public spaces, and the park would redefine the standard.

Once Walt established high expectations with his audience, he then sought to surprise us by exceeding the very expectations he had set. Exceeding our expectations is what makes the parks so appealing and why we keep coming back again and again. According to Gennawey, "A visit to Disneyland reassures us that things will be okay. Here, everything works, places can be clean, people can be nice, and the pace of the world feels right."

Regardless of where you are in your journey toward success, you can raise your expectations by first raising your standards for your surroundings. This is what Walt did with Disneyland, as noted by historian Judith Adams, "Everything about the park, including the behavior of the 'guests', is engineered to promote a spirit of optimism, a belief in progressive improvement toward perfection."

Believe in yourself and your ability to improve. Dreams may be messy, but that is no excuse for living in a mess. Engineer your expectations by enveloping yourself in an environment that encourages the success you are seeking. In her book *You Are a Badass at Making Money*, Jen Sincero says it this way:

We are energetic beings driven by emotion, so if your surroundings depress you, it's critical that you do whatever you can to brighten things up. Slap on a fresh coat of paint, clean your windows. . .get some plants, tidy up your clutter, throw a nice bedspread over your ratty couch, and if you've got sheets thumbtacked over the windows, please get some curtains.

"Just because you're trash doesn't mean you can't do great things. It is called garbage can, not garbage cannot."

— Oscar the Grouch

TRAVELING LIGHT

MY SEVENTY-EIGHT-YEAR-OLD DAD CAME TO California for a visit last year. Stories from that one visit could fill an entire book, but in the interest of keeping it clean and maintaining focus, I will limit us to three. Get ready to dive, Dad. You are about to go under!

First, my dad and step-mom traveled 2,000 miles to spend seven days in Southern California—a second honeymoon for them—with no baggage. For the record, I don't think it is possible to be married any length of time and not have baggage, but I digress. After greetings and hugs at the airport, I asked my dad how much luggage we needed to retrieve from baggage claim. My dad held up a small carry-on and, loud enough for all of LAX to hear proclaimed, "No bags, son! It's just Libby and me. Traveling light!" My dad was proud that he had avoided the twenty-five-dollar-per-piece luggage fee. I was proud that I bit my tongue and never told him, until now, that he was flying on Southwest Airlines where "bags fly free."

On the way home, Libby asked whether we could stop at Target so she could pick up toothpaste. Four hours and $400 later, our "light travelers" were ready, finally, to head to our house for lunch...except now it was so late that what Niki had planned as a light lunch would have to be dinner.

The next day, we took them into Hollywood. My dad had been to Southern California once, in 1960, for a trip to Disneyland. Fifty-five years later, he was shocked to see so many mountains surrounding Los Angeles.

"Son, I swear these mountains weren't here when your mom and I visited back in 1960."

"Well, you know dad, it's possible that Southern California has added mountains since the last time you were here," I responded.

"No, son. It's not possible just to add mountains somewhere," he stated.

"Sure, it is," I replied. "They've added Matterhorn Mountain, Space Mountain, Big Thunder Mountain, and Splash Mountain since the last time you were here!"

Dad wasn't amused with his smart-aleck son. Eventually, we realized that my dad missed the mountains during his first visit because he couldn't see them—the smog made it impossible. Thanks to the efforts of environmentalists, the air in Southern California is a lot cleaner than it once was. When it comes to the earth, keeping things clean isn't personal or political. It's global.

Lastly, my dad insisted on wearing a fanny pack into the parks—complete with wallet, change, keys, sunscreen, hat, poncho, snacks, and double-barreled water bottles. Getting through security with his utility belt was a nightmare. Walking him through the park turnstiles was worse. When my dad's fanny, and pack, became lodged in the logs at Splash Mountain, forcing everything to spill out, I was Zip-A-Dee-Doo-Dah-DONE! We returned to the hotel for an afternoon nap, but before we returned to the park, I banned the fanny pack. I promised my dad that I would buy him anything he could possibly need, when he needed it. Carrying all this crap around was threatening to ruin the whole experience. At least for me.

It is good to want things. It keeps you motivated.

But the more you have, the more you must clean, carry, and maintain. Americans today have way too much "stuff." We witness this reality every time we walk into a Disney park and see the hordes of super-size shopping bags and SUV-sized strollers. In March 2017, Robert Niles, at the website Theme Park Insider, sparked controversy in Southern California when he wrote an article titled, "What should Disneyland do about its swarm of strollers?" Niles knows what all of us have noticed— the problem isn't the number of children or strollers. The problem is the size of the strollers. He writes:

[U]ltimately, the problem isn't the number of children in Disneyland. It's the size of those darned strollers these days. Perhaps Disneyland could divert some of Walt Disney World's "NextGen" money into designing and developing the next generation of smaller, stronger, more durable strollers, which Disney could rent in place of its current, somewhat bulky models.

Of course, that wouldn't do anything to address the much larger, SUV-sized rolling roadblocks that many parents are bringing into the park. To do that, Disney would have to get really devious and start emulating...the airline industry.

Wanna bring a stroller into the park? Like checking a bag on a flight, you're gonna have to pay. Let's make the daily stroller admission fee equal to the daily stroller rental fee. That way, people are paying the same whether they bring their own or use Disney's (in our ideal world) smaller strollers.

Must use your own? Then you might have to pay an oversized stroller penalty on top of the stroller admission fee, just as you would for an overweight checked bag on an airline trip.

Why do people bring in such big strollers, anyway? Because for many families, the issue isn't a place to stash the kid.

It's having a place to stash *their stuff*. People need the big strollers to accommodate the diaper bag, backpacks, snack bags, and whatever else they're hauling into the park like they were preparing to climb Mount Everest.

If you want to enjoy life, travel light. Disneyland, and my dad, will thank you.

"A great many of us are possessed by our possessions."

— Mildred Lisette Norman

EATING CLEAN

Soon after Niki and I moved into our new home in Southern California, Bethany and her boyfriend came for a visit. Both were just out of college and transitioning into full adulthood, which included learning to cook. They had spent the previous months experimenting and perfecting a few culinary delights, so they were excited to share their newfound talents with us by insisting that they prepare dinner one evening.

Niki and I readily agreed. We were buoyed by their maturity and sudden recognition that they couldn't spend the rest of their days eating cereal, Pop Tarts, or hanging out every evening at an all-night Denny's. Plus, while Niki is an amazing cook, she can certainly use a night off every now and then.

As Bethany and beau took over, our kitchen exploded into a scene that looked like the lost holiday shipment scattered around the jungle in Magic Kingdom's annual Jingle Cruise overlay. Supper stuff was *everywhere.*

"Don't worry about the mess," Bethany proclaimed. "This dish is amazing. We will get everything cleaned up after dinner."

Several hours later, we sat down to the gourmet grub spread before us. Famished, we plowed into our plates, only to discover that something had gone terribly wrong. I looked around at my fellow diners who all had the same, quizzical look on their faces. By the third bite, I jumped up and shouted, "I can't take it anymore. Why does this dish taste like soap?"

Everyone dropped their forks and exclaimed, "Thank God! I thought it was just me."

Fearing the worst, Niki asked Bethany what she had used for the sauté. Bethany walked over to the kitchen sink and held up the "olive oil" jar which, unbeknownst to her, Niki was using as the soap dispenser in our new house.

"Ugh!" we all screamed.

"Eating clean" may be the latest diet and nutrition fad, but having your supper sautéed in soap is taking things to the extreme.

And that's my point. Don't let keeping things clean and well-maintained turn into obsessive, compulsive perfectionism. Perfect doesn't exist, even for Disneyland. When the park opened, it impressed everyone with its cleanliness. But it was far from "perfect."

For example, one of my favorite stops in our History of Disneyland tour is on Main Street at Coke Corner. Here I like to point out a red-and-white lightbulb known as "Walt's Lightbulb." Overhead is a series of alternating red and white bulbs, but the odd shape of the space requires an odd number of bulbs. The story goes that breaking the alternating red-and-white pattern drove Walt nuts, so one night, he grabbed a paintbrush and painted the last bulb half-red and half-white.

Whew! I thought my mom had issues!

In his efforts to make Disneyland a perfect utopia, perhaps Walt forgot the words of his good friend, Salvador Dali, who reminds us, "Have no fear of perfection. You'll never attain it."

When it comes to dreams and success, waiting for everything to be just right before you get started means you never will. At some point, you must: Start. Launch. Go. I am giving you permission to be *imperfect.* You will make your mistakes along the way. That's okay, as long as you clean up your own messes.

And bring your own olive oil.

And paint your own light bulbs.

> *"Perfectionism makes you stay home, not take chances,*
> *and procrastinate on projects; it makes you think your life is*
> *worse than it is; it keeps you from being yourself;*
> *it stress you out; it tells you that good is bad; and it ignores*
> *the natural way in which things work.*
>
> — Stephen Guise

SOUVENIR STOP

MAKE YOUR BED—MY MOTHER'S OBSESSION with neatness started at the beginning of each day. We were never allowed to leave our rooms until we had made our beds. Again, she wasn't wrong.

In a commencement speech at the University of Texas at Austin, Navy Admiral William McRaven schooled graduates on the importance of making your bed each morning:

1. From the start of the day you will have already accomplished your first task of the day.
2. This small sense of accomplishment, and the ensuing sense of pride, will encourage you to do another task. And another. "By the end of the day, that one task completed will have turned into many tasks completed."
3. Making your bed is also a reminder that little things matter. Worst-case scenario, no matter how bad your day becomes, you will have a made bed to come home to and a chance to start anew the next day.

Good advice from a Special Operations Commander and the man who was head of the Joint Special Operations Command during the Osama bin Laden raid in 2011—or, if you are my mom, a woman trying to survive a house being overrun by four small children.

"As you make your bed, so you must lie in it."

— Daniel J. Boosting

ENERGIZE YOUR ENVIRONMENT—WE FEEL BETTER at a Disney park because Disney does the dirty work for us. Commit to being an adult by taking responsibility for your success and upgrading your surroundings. How will you improve the following seven areas over the upcoming week?

1. Your home? _____

_____

2. Your office? _____

_____

3. Your car? _____

_____

4. Your wardrobe? _____

_____

5. Your eating habits? _____

_____

6. Your music? _____

_____

7. Your language? _____

_____

> *"Shabby is as shabby does."*
>
> — Jen Sincero

A CLEAN SWEEP—IF YOU WANT to get serious about being a light traveler, then read Marie Kondo's international bestselling book, *The Life-Changing Magic of Tidying Up*. The "lite" version of the book is below:

1. Start by discarding all at once, intensely and completely.
2. Keep only those things that speak to your heart.
3. The question of what you want to own is actually the question of how you want to live your life.

> *"The space in which we live should be for the person we are becoming now, not for the person we were in the past."*
>
> — Marie Kondo

GETTING YOUR HAND STAMPED

WHEN WALT BUILT DISNEYLAND, HE insisted that a trash can be available to guests every thirty steps. Why thirty steps? Because Walt's favorite food was a hot dog, so he measured out how many steps it took him to eat his favorite treat before finishing and looking for a trash can to toss the wrapper. To this day, this is the standard that every Disney park follows.

Disney takes its trash cans so seriously because it takes keeping the parks clean seriously. When Walt Disney World opened in 1971, a trash can cost an average of $1,500. Why so much? Because, according to Koenig, "Every trash can was decorated to blend with its surroundings, such as being hand-painted to resemble bamboo in Adventureland or logs in Frontierland." Yet, even at $1,500 each, not every can in the Kingdom is created equal.

Starting in 1995, Florida's Tomorrowland was home to a special trash can named "Push." Push was a silver-and-blue Audio-Animatronics can that talked and interacted with guests. Over the years, Push participated in several marriage proposals, danced with celebrities (his greatest thrill was dancing with Michael Jackson), and unofficially ran for political office as the Mayor of Tomorrowland. Disney fans adored him.

But all good things must come to an end. After nineteen years of service, Push was canned. Most guests viewed the loss of Push a waste, but Lou Mangello of WDW Radio put it into perspective when he told the *New York Daily News*, "[I]t is a loss but Walt Disney World is not a museum. It's an ever-changing animal."

If you are looking to push yourself to the next level of success, start by keeping what you already have clean and well-maintained. Be an ever-changing animal by making the full transition from childhood to adulthood and take responsibility for maintaining your stuff. Clean out your museum and surround yourself only with the things you truly love.

Travel Light.

"Walt never lived in Orlando. He only visited the town a few times before his death. Yet his vision and values have made Orlando what it is today—a city unlike any other. You sense it in the optimistic spirit of the people you meet. You see it in the clean, broad streets and beautifully designed buildings. Walt's spirit is alive in this town."

— Pat Williams and Jim Denney

LEAVING A LEGACY

*"Think beyond your lifetime if you want to accomplish
something truly worthwhile."*

— Walt Disney

MR. TOAD'S LAST RIDE

SEPTEMBER 7, 1998 WAS A sad day at Walt Disney World's Magic
Kingdom. This was the day that Mr. Toad, a rare opening day attraction
for both Disneyland and Walt Disney World, took its final ride, *to
nowhere in particular,* in Florida. As an attraction, Mr. Toad has always
been a bit different. For Disneyland, it was the closest the park came to
having a thrill ride on opening day. Per Sam Gennawey in *The Disneyland
Story,* the preliminary plans called for Mr. Toad to be a "roller coaster
with the cars following a downhill track towards obstacles that would
move out of the way at the last minute." Walt worried, however, that
the ride might be too rough so he insisted that they tone Toad down.
Nonetheless, the attraction does feature a manor, a motorcar, and a
madcap journey that takes guests on a great adventure of mischief and
mayhem. Everything ends abruptly when guests collide with a train
and are hastened to hell.

Concerned that East Coast guests would complain if they did not
get to enjoy the same Fantasyland stories found at Disneyland, the

version of Mr. Toad that was once found in Florida follows well Roy's thinking that opening day attractions in the Magic Kingdom should remain true to Walt's originals in California but still be slightly different. As such, Snow White, Peter Pan, and Mr. Toad all found their way to Florida in 1971 with Mr. Toad housing the most obvious and significant differences. The original in Disneyland shares squeezed space in the same building with both Peter Pan's Flight and Alice in Wonderland, but Florida's Mr. Toad would feature an expanded version that included separate tracks, separate boarding areas, separate ride experiences, and the illusion that vehicles on the different tracks were heading toward each other and a collision was imminent.

The reaction to Mr. Toad's demise is interesting, especially in contrast to the closing of another attraction in Fantasyland just a few years earlier. You will remember from a previous chapter the story of the closing of 20,000 Leagues Under the Sea. When that attraction closed on September 5, 1994, it did so for "maintenance" and it was only announced *later* that this was a terminal closure and that the subs would never surface again. Heartbroken, legions of fans lamented that they never had an opportunity for a last ride.

"If only we had known," they cried.

"If only we could have said our goodbyes," they screamed.

Desiring to avoid the despondency they faced over the demise of the beloved submarines, Disney announced on October 22, 1997 that Toad would be toast on September 7, 1998. Fan reaction was as predictable as the five stages of grief, except fans skipped denial and went straight to anger. A "Save the Toad" movement sprung up overnight, and for the next eleven months, Disney had to deal with postcards, letters, demonstrations, and even sit-ins on the attraction that the media dubbed as "Toad-Ins."

As a person who has both pastored *and* worked as a professional in the funeral industry (*not* the happiest place on Earth), I have seen the same response to death. When a loved one dies without notice, i.e., the unannounced closure of 20,000 Leagues Under the Sea, we lament the loss by wishing we had known in advance and could have said goodbye. When, however, a loved one passes following a lengthy terminal illness, i.e., Mr. Toad, many wish it had been more sudden and the suffering of the previous months had never happened.

Both approaches miss the point.

Death sucks.

We all prepare for vacations, yet few of us prepare to vacate.

None of us wants to think about the inevitable imminence of our own demise. None of us wants to face the fact that we are "foolish mortals." Death is the one line we are all waiting in, and yet nobody is asking for a fast pass. To quote country recording artist Kenny Chesney, "Everybody wants to go to heaven, but nobody wants to go now."

But go we must.

One day, a carriage *will* approach to take you from this world and into the next. One of the best ways to prepare is by planning now for the legacy you will leave behind. And yes, the parks give us an example of how to do this as well.

NO ATTRACTION LEFT BEHIND

By DEFINITION, DREAMERS DESIRE TO make a dent in the world. All of us want to know that our ideas, thoughts, and efforts matter. We want to make a memorable difference.

As a professor, I have spent two decades teaching courses and reading student evaluations of me and my classes at the end of each semester. I learned early on to read these reviews as if they are from Olympic figure-skating judges—some students will love you, others will hate you, and somewhere in the middle lies the story of the overall student experience and my performance for that class and that semester. I value the feedback, but I have become immune to the roller coaster of emotions that will ensue if I succumb to the comments found on the extremes.

Until recently.

Last year, I was in downtown Riverside when I ran into a couple of CBU students. One of them knew me, but the other responded with "I think we've met before. In fact, I may have had you in a history class a couple of years ago."

May?

May have had me in a history class a couple of years ago?

I pride myself on being memorable. You can love me. You can hate me. But please, please, please don't forget me.

The same goes for death. None of us is getting out of here alive. But how will we be remembered? What kind of legacy can we leave? Will anyone ever know we were ever even here?

At the Disney parks, our old favorites may well be gone, but they need not be forgotten. In fact, there is a long list of legacy reminders from former attractions that exist in current ones. Our first example comes from Mr. Toad himself at Walt Disney World. In Florida, the rationale for Toad reaching the end of the road rests in the ride that replaced him. Where Toad once stood now stands The Many Adventures of Winnie the Pooh. Mr. Toad originates from a rather obscure Disney 1949 "package" film, *The Adventures of Ichabod and Mr. Toad*. With the opening of Epcot and the introduction of the all-inclusive ticket, it was no longer necessary for individual attractions to generate revenue directly. By the 1990s, "synergy," or "cross-merchandising" is what mattered. Poor Mr. Toad doesn't have much to offer in this regard. However, Winnie-the Pooh, the rights to which Disney acquired in the 1960s, is a "merchandising juggernaut worth billions annually." Thus, on June 4, 1999, The Many Adventures of Winnie the Pooh opened as the replacement for Mr. Toad's Wild Ride in Walt Disney World's Magic Kingdom.

Ironically enough, British author A. A. Milne not only created Pooh but he wrote the play version of Kenneth Grahame's novel *The Wind in the Willows*, in which Toad is the main character. It is fitting, therefore, that today one can find a tribute to Toad inside Pooh—a mural image showing Mr. Toad handing the deed for Toad Hall to Owl—the wise old friend of Winnie the Pooh and resident know-it-all in the Hundred Acre Wood. In addition, you can also visit Toad's grave marker as you exit the Haunted Mansion and pass by the pet cemetery.

These sorts of "remembrances" are evident throughout the Disney parks. It is common for Imagineers to pay tribute to former attractions by including memories of "what once was" in the newer attractions that replace them. Examples include:

DISNEYLAND

The Many Adventures of Winnie the Pooh—Back in 2004, Pooh displaced the California version of the Country Bears. Nonetheless, Max the Deer, Melvin the Moose, and Buff the Buffalo still hang overhead just after the Heffalumps and Woozles scene. Look back and up to view.

Indiana Jones Adventure—To construct the ginormous queue and show building for Indy, Imagineers had to take out a portion of the original Disneyland parking lot so the old Eeyore section disappeared long before tourists to the temple started vanishing. The Eeyore sign from the parking lot is hidden high in the projector room. When experiencing the attraction, you must avoid looking into the eyes of Mara, but be sure to keep an eye out for Eeyore!

MAGIC KINGDOM

Seven Dwarfs Mine Train—In 2012, Disney did away with another original dark ride from opening day. Snow White's Scary Adventures may be no more, but Seven Dwarfs Mine Train shares the same Snow White story *and* the vultures overhead were vultured from the original ride.

Under the Sea—Journey of the Little Mermaid—This attraction sits where the lagoon for 20,000 Leagues Under the Sea once lay. Both attractions aim for the same goal—to take you under the sea, complete with mermaids! Less obvious is the cleverly hidden outline of a Nautilus submarine that Imagineers etched into the rock work around the Ariel attraction.

Tomorrowland Transit Authority PeopleMover—Aside from reminding us of the mode of transportation Walt envisioned for EPCOT and housing the model of Progress City, the PeopleMover also broadcasts this legacy language while you are riding inside Space Mountain, "Paging Mr. Morrow, Mr. Tom Morrow, please contact Mr. Johnson to confirm your flight to the moon." Tom Morrow is obviously a reference to Tomorrowland and Mr. Johnson used to host the former Flight to the Moon and Mission to Mars attractions.

EPCOT

Mission Space—Mission Space replaced the beloved Horizons attraction in 2003. You can still look for the Horizons logo throughout Mission Space, to include the rotating gravity wheel in both the Mission Space queue and gift shop. Mission Space also makes room for tributes to both Mission to Mars and Flight to the Moon from Magic Kingdom.

Frozen—In 2016, Frozen replaced Maelstrom as the featured attraction inside the Norway Pavilion. Puffins from the original ride remain, however, along with a painting of three Maelstrom trolls inside the adjacent Anna and Elsa Meet and Greet area.

HOLLYWOOD STUDIOS

Star Tours—The original Star Tours opened at Disneyland in 1987 and then found its way to Florida, via Hollywood Studios, in late 1989. Both versions were upgraded in 2011 as Star Tours—The Adventure Continues. Remnants of the original "Flight to Endor" remain, including Captain Rex, who, in accordance with the sacred Star Wars timeline, has not yet been used and is being shipped back to the factory as "defective."

*"If you would not be forgotten as soon as you are dead,
either write something worth reading
or do things worth writing."*

— Benjamin Franklin

ISLANDS OF INTENTION

IN OUR REVIEW OF TRIBUTES to old attractions, you may have noticed the absence of Animal Kingdom, the fourth and final theme park constructed at Walt Disney World. This is due in part to the fact that the park is the newest (less than twenty years old) and home to more animals than attractions. In other words, nothing has needed to be replaced at this point.

The park does, however, remind us of an even more important legacy lesson. Today, Animal Kingdom is as famous for what "never was" than anything that has come and gone. Part of the original plans for Animal Kingdom included a fascinating section called "Beastly Kingdom." Beastly Kingdom was to be divided into both an "Evil Realm" and a "Good Realm." Jeff Kurti, in the twenty-fifth anniversary book celebrating the opening of Walt Disney World, *Since the World Began,* describes Beastly Kingdom as follows:

> In this mythical world of unicorns, dragons, and other magical creatures, guests will come face to face with make believe animals from legends, fairy tales, and storybooks— all of which play an important role in the circle of life because of their powerful hold on our imagination.

Unfortunately, creating an animal kingdom with actual animals is very costly. For example, Kilimanjaro Safari may be only "one" attraction, but it is more than 100 acres in size—equivalent to Florida's entire Magic Kingdom. Because of ballooning budgets, Beastly Kingdom was put on hold and planned for "Phase Two" with an announced construction date of no later than 2003.

In the interim, Universal opened its second Orlando park, Islands of Adventure in 1999. If you look at the original plans for Beastly Kingdom and then visit Islands of Adventure, you will see some striking similarities. The Lost Continent is a land built around the motif of "myths and legends." With a decrepit medieval castle serving as its queue, Dueling Dragons is a dual-tracked, inverted roller coaster. On opening day, there was even a kiddie coaster, The Flying Unicorn (since re-themed for Harry Potter to Flight of the Hippogriff).

Disney was dismayed at the development. According to Christopher E. Smith in *The Walt Disney World That Never Was: Stories Behind the Amazing Imagineering Dreams That Never Came True*, "[T]here was no way that Disney executives, especially Eisner, were going to move forward with a land based on myth and legend when Universal had already done exactly that."

References to Beastly Kingdom, the land and dream that never was, are abundant in Animal Kingdom. There is a "unicorn" prancing on signs in a section of the park's parking lot. Look closely at the park's logo and you will find five silhouettes with a dragon featured in the center.

The road to nowhere—*nowhere in particular*—is paved with good intentions. When you reach the end of your road, you want to be remembered for what you *did*. Not for what you *didn't* do.

The book you *never* wrote.

The business you *never* started.

The trip you *never* took.

The words you *never* spoke.

After teaching my dream course, The History of Disneyland, surviving brain surgery, and returning to work in Fall 2014, I commented to Niki that it was nice that I could teach the class, but my real dream was to write a leadership and success book based on Disneyland.

"If I had died from the tumor, my only regret would have been that I never wrote my book. A book I have been thinking about since 1991," I told Niki.

"Wow, if that is your *only* regret at fifty-one years of age, you are doing better than most," Niki replied. Then she followed with, "So, what do we need to do now to make that dream a reality?"

The success of *The Wisdom of Walt* has exceeded my wildest expectations. As the months unfolded, I came to realize that the message was bigger than me (and I am kind of a *big* deal). I now know that the book will continue to live on well past my own mortal lifetime. Other than my children, who will one day perish as well, *The Wisdom of Walt* will be my legacy. I am amazed by the feedback I receive from readers. One woman was motivated to lose fifty pounds after reading the book; others have quit their ho-hum jobs to go work for Disney. One couple sold their home and is living their dream, in an RV, traveling the country. In that vein, and to encourage and inspire you toward your dream and legacy, I want to share with you a letter from a reader:

Mr. Barnes—

Or Dr. Disneyland, or Jeffrey, or any other moniker you may wish to go by—

I'm writing you this email to let you know that I just finished reading your book and I absolutely loved it. I first heard about it when you were interviewed for the Dis Unplugged podcast and immediately asked for a copy for Christmas. I'm glad I did.

It isn't easy for me to say this, but I suffer from depression and am currently fighting for a dream job in the entertainment industry. Self-motivation and confidence are not in my nature. It's all too easy for my inner critic to talk me out of fighting for my goals. But Walt Disney has been a hero and enormous inspiration to me since childhood and Disneyland is the one place on earth where my depression can't reach me.

When I first heard about your book, I admit, I was skeptical. But the way you framed those important life lessons, in a way I could understand and appreciate, made the book more enjoyable to read. I did one chapter a day, just enough for me to dwell on each lesson, and I know that what I learned is going to come in handy.

I live on the East Coast, as far away from Disneyland as you can get in this country, but reading your book made me feel like I was there. It was nothing short of inspirational.

So thanks, Mr. Barnes. Thanks for sharing your wisdom and the Wisdom of Walt.

Shortly after releasing *The Wisdom of Walt* in July 2015, I embarked on a speaking tour to promote the book and get the message out to as many people as possible. Less than a year later, I found myself presenting at a corporate event in the Connecticut cold of February. I built my message around Mastering Walt Disney's 4 Cs of Success: Curiosity, Confidence, Courage, and Constancy.

I spoke that night about courage and how Walt faced all kinds of demons and dragons as he battled to make his dream of Disneyland a reality. I also shared how I was diagnosed with a brain tumor the day after my dream, teaching a college course on The History of Disneyland, had started. I used these stories to remind the audience that every story needs a hero; every dream needs someone to step up and take the lead.

"If not you, then who? If not now, then when?" I challenged.

After the event, I was signing books when a man came up and asked whether I would sign his copy—not for him but for his wife.

"Of course," I replied. "What's her name?"

With a tear in his eye, he replied, "My wife's name is Maureen. We've been married for more than forty years and she is a *huge* Disney fan. She is currently battling breast cancer, and my Maureen could sure use a shot of courage tonight."

I left that event not thinking about how many books I had sold or how my speech had gone, but hoping simply that my book would give Maureen the courage to fight on. That her husband thought I could help was in itself worth all the time and work of writing that book.

> *"Life should not be a journey to the grave with the intention of arriving safely in a pretty and well preserved body, but rather to skid in broadside in a cloud of smoke, thoroughly used up, totally worn out, and loudly proclaiming "Wow! What a ride!"*

— Hunter S. Thompson

SOUVENIR STOP

MEMENTO MORI—THE HAUNTED MANSION IS one of Disney's most beloved attractions and the only ride constructed simultaneously for both Disneyland and Walt Disney World. Anaheim's opened in August 1969 and Florida's was found as an opening day attraction in 1971. Imagineers in Glendale constructed two of almost everything—installing pieces for Anaheim as they went and keeping props for Walt Disney World until it was time to fly them to Florida.

Throughout the ride and associated souvenir shops, you will find the words "*Memento Mori*." It is featured on tombstones, trinkets, and T-shirts. Nearly every Disney fan has seen the words, but do you know what they mean? *Memento Mori* is Latin for "Remember that you have to die."

When it comes to your legacy, it is wise to "remember that you have to die." You don't have forever, and time is your only non-renewable resource. Many of us use "countdown" apps for events we are looking forward to; for example, Niki and I are taking our first Disney Cruise in July 2017. This morning it is only 160 days away!

In the spirit of *Memento Mori*, why not approach your inevitable departure the same way? There are numerous websites, apps, and other resources that will take your health, family history, habits, etc., and using actuary tables, calculate how many days you have left. Personally, I used fatefinder.com until that website met its fate and disappeared from the Internet. It is a sobering exercise, but I am scheduled to check out on May 2, 2042—less than 10,000 days left!

"Your cadaverous pallor betrays an aura of foreboding,
almost as though you sense a disquieting metamorphosis."

— Ghost Host at The Haunted Mansion

PUT YOU IN YOUR EULOGY—PSYCHOLOGISTS have shown that asking people how they would like to be remembered after their deaths has a motivational effect on long-term goals and lifelong aspirations. This forces us to "look alive" and puts the power of *now* in perspective.

So, how would *you* like to be remembered? I am going to challenge you to make this dismaying observation. Imagine for a moment that your closest friend is standing up at your funeral and delivering *your* ideal eulogy. How would you want him or her to describe:

1. Your personality? _____

_____

_____

2. Your achievements? _____
_____
_____

3. Your personal strengths? _____
_____
_____

4. Your family life? _____
_____
_____

5. Your professional success? _____
_____
_____

6. Behavior toward others? _____
_____
_____

This exercise is borrowed from Richard Wiseman's book, *59 Seconds: Think a Little, Change a Lot*. End the exercise with this question, "Do your present behaviors justify the comments, or is there work to be done?"

"A good ending is vital to a picture,
the single most important element, because it is what
the audience takes with them out of the theatre."

— Walt Disney

GETTING YOUR HAND STAMPED

THE YEAR 2016, WHEN THE bulk of this book was written, was a year filled with famous deaths. For me, it started on January 18 with the passing of Rock 'n' Roll Hall-of-Famer, Glenn Frey. In July 1971, Linda Ronstadt was doing a week-long gig at Disneyland and hired Don Henley, Bernie Leadon, Randy Meisner, and Frey as her backup band. This is the first time the four had ever played together, and they enjoyed the experience so much that they went on to form the legendary group, The Eagles, my all-time favorite band.

The year ended with the back-to-back deaths of Carrie Fisher and her beloved mom, Debbie Reynolds, on December 29 and 30—within twenty-four hours of each other. Carrie, of course, played Princess Leia in the Star Wars film franchise. Debbie Reynolds was a star in her own right and was photographed alongside her husband, Eddie Fisher, with Walt himself on the opening day of Disneyland, July 17, 1955.

In the middle of 2016, July 2, was another death that at first glance might not seem Disney-related. Elie Wiesel was a Holocaust survivor, Nobel laureate, and Nobel Peace Prize winner. After surviving both Auschwitz and Buchenwald, Wiesel aspired to become a journalist and even interviewed Walt Disney in France at the 1953 Cannes Film Festival. He arrived in America in 1955, the same year Disneyland opened, and then made a fateful visit to "The Happiest Place on Earth" in 1957. His trip was part of a six-week cross-country sojourn while recovering from injuries related to being hit by a car in Manhattan's Times Square.

Wiesel was so wowed by Disneyland that he would go on to write about it in his Yiddish column for *The Forverts* where he was a regular contributor. His reflections on Walt's Magic Kingdom mirror what so many feel, but few find the words to express:

> I don't know if a Garden of Eden awaits adults in the hereafter. I do know, though, that there is a Garden of

Eden for children here in this life. I know because I myself visited this paradise. I have just returned from there, just passed through its gates, just left the magical kingdom known as Disneyland. And as I bid that kingdom farewell, I understood for the first time the true meaning of the French saying, "to leave is to die a little" (*parter, c'est mourir in peu*).

In 1955, a decade after the end of World War II and the discovery of the death camps in Europe, the world needed Walt Disney because the world needed Disneyland. More than sixty years later, a dream that began as a crazy thought on a park bench one Saturday afternoon lives on in Disney parks around the world—with the Magic Kingdom in Florida being the first replication.

Today, the world needs you and your dream. What will your legacy be? How will you be remembered? What kind of dent might your dream possibly make? You won't know, and neither will we, unless you get started.

Now.

Yes, you might die a little along the way. But please, don't leave this world without at least trying. *Memento Mori*—your clock is ticking.

> *"Today, the sun never sets on the operation of*
> *a Disney park somewhere in the world."*

> — Marty Sklar
> Former Vice President of Walt Disney Imagineering,
> Disney Legend, and the Only Person to Attend
> Opening Day Ceremonies for All Twelve Disney Parks

CONCLUSION
SEE YA' REAL SOON!

As you exit Walt Disney World, you see the opposite side of the same sign you passed under when you entered. This side, however, says, "See Ya' Real Soon!" This famous closing line to *The Mickey Mouse Club* TV series serves as a reminder that the world is big enough for you to return to and repeat your favorite experiences and explore new adventures not yet realized.

What I want to see is *your* dreams come true—real soon!

When the dream of Walt Disney World became reality in October 1971, Disney celebrated with a nationally televised broadcast on its *Wonderful World of Disney* television show. The star-studded gala included Glen Campbell, Julie Andrews, and Bob Hope. Hope, arriving by monorail, spoke inside the Contemporary Resort and gave a moving tribute to his friend, Walt Disney:

> Walt Disney believed in the beauty and natural wonders of the world. But he felt that as we passed through that we should try to add a little wonder and beauty to it. Maybe you'll understand that Walt's dream was just a beginning. The dream doesn't stop here. This is the start of it....

My hope is that this book has provided you with stories and strategies that will get you motivated and get you moving. But reading *Beyond the Wisdom of Walt* is just a beginning. Your dream doesn't stop here. This is the start!

So what's next?

Action!

The most important step you can take on your way to success and seeing your own dreams come true is to take action, any action, in the direction you know you want to go. Regardless of where you are, there is always a way forward. This is what Walt Disney taught us—but not at Disneyland or Walt Disney World. He taught us this back in 1923 in Kansas City, Missouri. There, after losing his first studio, Laugh O' Gram Studio, to bankruptcy, he made the difficult decision to go *all in* on his dream of being an animator. Walt boarded a train bound for California. He boarded this train with forty dollars, a single suitcase, and a one-way ticket. This decision changed his world—and ours.

What decision does your dream need?

I know you are scared. Every dream is scary. But the only thing scarier is staying stuck and not even trying.

The Wisdom of Walt began with the story of Walt Disney sitting on a park bench on a Saturday afternoon while his daughters, Diane and Sharon, rode the merry-go-round at Griffith Park in Los Angeles. It was there, on that bench, that he first dreamed of a place where "parents and children could have fun together."

Imagine for a moment that you are there on that important day. Here is what scares me. *What if Walt Disney never gets up off of that bench? What if Walt Disney never believes in himself and his dream? What if Walt Disney never builds Disneyland or Walt Disney World?*

The model for EPCOT that Walt wanted to build, his Experimental Prototype Community of Tomorrow, included park benches. Walt had already picked out his bench and often showed it to others, exclaiming that it was there, on his bench, that he would retire. He looked forward to living out his final days with Lilly, inside his final dream, as they sat together watching people go by inside the world that he created.

But the future can be cruel sometimes. Walt never made it to Disney World so his version of EPCOT was never realized. None of us has forever.

It is past time for you to take your dreams seriously. Stop sitting on your park bench and start changing your world. I can't wait to see what you do next.

See Ya' Real Soon.

"Laughter is timeless. Imagination has no age.
And dreams are forever."

— Walt Disney

Jeff and Niki celebrating the completion of *Beyond the Wisdom of Walt,* July 2017

ACKNO@LEDGMENTS

J<small>UST AS</small> M<small>AIN</small> S<small>TREET</small>, U.S.A. gives credit to the people at Disney who helped make the parks possible, I want to take a moment and thank the members of my team who helped make *The Wisdom of Walt* a success and *Beyond the Wisdom of Walt* possible.

First, to the readers and fans of *The Wisdom of Walt* who let me know how much the message meant to you and how the book motivated and inspired you to start following your dreams, thank you. Without your encouragement, I never would have dared to dream of writing a second book. Hopefully, *Beyond the Wisdom of Walt* lives up to your expectations. You can let me know whether I need to write a third. *The Worldwide Wisdom of Walt,* perhaps?

Thank you to my wife, Niki, for bearing with me through this process all over again. Your edits, comments, critique, and encouragement are always appreciated. Our life together wouldn't be possible without you. I also want to acknowledge our children, Bethany, Logan, and Wesley. Thank you for allowing me to share some of our stories. And an apology to my "Alter/Walter Ego," Albert for not making it into this book. Maybe next time, buddy.

I also want to express my appreciation to California Baptist University for its uncompromising support of my History of Disneyland class and the encouragement to keep writing. I especially appreciate the support from Dr. Chuck Sands and Dr. Tracy Ward. Thank you.

Once again, my team in the Office of Student Success deserves more than a few words of thanks and appreciation. *Beyond the Wisdom of Walt* would never have been possible without input from Steve "The Captain" Neilsen, Mike Osadchuck, Pam Jost, Sheri Torelli, and Jennifer Lee.

I also want to say a word of thanks to my editor, Tyler Tichelaar. You have the ability to take something that is okay and make it terrific. Thank you for understanding what I wanted to say even when I did not know how to say it. I also appreciate your willingness to continue schooling me on split infinitives, how to write dialogue, and why I don't want to use All Caps and scream at my readers. THANK YOU, TYLER!

Beyond the Wisdom of Walt was a true team effort. Thank you Patrick Snow for being there at the beginning, and to Nicole Gabriel, Kyle Ready, and Choi Messer for your great graphic work, cover designs, and interior layouts. You are all, as always, awesome!

Lastly, I want to say a special thank you to my other Disney authors. First, to Marty Sklar, who sadly passed away just before this book went to press. He will be greatly missed. The stories and history found in this book stand on the work done by Marty as well as David Koenig, Jim Korkis, Sam Gennawey, Pat Williams, Jim Denney, and many others. If you have not yet read their work, do yourself a favor and go get their books. You will be glad you did!

ABOUT THE AUTHOR

JEFF BARNES IS THE BEST-SELLING author of *The Wisdom of Walt: Leadership Lessons from the Happiest Place on Earth* and *Beyond the Wisdom of Walt: Life Lessons from the Most Magical Place on Earth*. Known as Dr. Disneyland, he teaches the only accredited college course on the History of Disneyland. He is an international speaker, higher education administrator, university professor, and leadership/success coach. He has more than thirty-five years of professional speaking experience and nearly twenty years' experience leading teams in higher education and teaching more than twenty different college courses.

He attributes his passion for Disney parks to his love of history, story, and success. He believes the parks teach us some of life's greatest lessons—as long as you know their history, you know what to look for, and you are willing to connect it all to your own story.

Jeff lives in Riverside, California with his family. When he is not speaking, teaching, or writing, Jeff enjoys spending as much time as possible in "The Happiest Place on Earth."

TELL ME ABOUT YOUR DREAM!

🌐 www.thewisdomofwalt.com
✉️ jeff@thewisdomofwalt.com
📘 Jeff Barnes *or* The Wisdom of Walt
📷 @drdisneyland
🐦 @drdisneyland

BIBLIOGRAPHY

BOOKS

Abrashoff, Capt. D. Michael. *Management Techniques from the Best Damn Ship in the Navy.* New York, NY: Business Plus, 2002.

Acuff, Jonathan. *Do Over: Make Today the First Day of Your New Career.* NY, NY: Portfolio/Penguin, 2017.

Acuff, Jonathan. *Start: Punch Fear in the Face, Escape Average and Do Work that Matters.* Brentwood, TN: Lampo Press, 2013.

Acuff, Jonathan M. *Quitter: Closing the Gap between Your Day Job & Your Dream Job.* Brentwood, TN: Lampo, The Lampo Group, 2011.

Altucher, James. *Choose Yourself: Be Happy, Make Millions, Live the Dream.* n.p.: 2016.

Barczewski, Stephanie. *Magic Kingdoms: A History of the Disney Theme Parks.* Orlando, FL: Theme Park Press, 2016.

Barrett, Steven M. *Disneyland's Hidden Mickeys: A Field Guide to Disneyland Resort's Best Kept Secrets.* Branford, CT: The Intrepid Traveler, 2013.

Beard, Richard R. *Walt Disney's EPCOT: Creating the New World of Tomorrow.* New York, NY: Harry N. Abrams, 1982.

Bright, Randy. *Disneyland: Inside Story.* New York, NY: Harry N. Abrams, Inc., 1987.

Broggie, Michael. *Walt Disney's Railroad Story.* Pasadena, CA: Pentrex, 1997.

Bryman, Alan. *Disney and His Worlds.* New York, NY: Routledge, 1995.

Canfield, Jack. *The Success Principles.* New York, NY: HarperCollins Publishers, 2005.

Capodagli, Bill and Lynn Jackson. *The Disney Way: Harnessing the*

Management Secrets of Disney in Your Company. New York, NY: McGraw-Hill, 2007.

Cardone, Grant. *Be Obsessed or Be Average.* New York: Portfolio/Penguin, 2016.

Cardone, Grant. *The Ten X Rule: The Only Difference between Success and Failure.* Hoboken, NJ: Wiley, 2011.

Catmull, Ed. *Creativity, Inc.: Overcoming the Unseen Forces That Stand in the Way of True Inspiration.* New York, NY: Random House, 2014.

Cockerell, Lee. *Creating Magic: 10 Common Sense Leadership Strategies from a Life at Disney.* New York, NY: Doubleday, 2008.

Cockerell, Lee. *The Customer Rules: The 39 Essential Rules for Delivering Sensational Service.* New York: Crown Business, 2013.

Cockerell, Lee. *Time Management Magic: How to Get More Done Every Day, Move from Surviving to Thriving.* Tulsa, OK: Emerge, 2014.

Crump, Rolly and Jeff Heimbuch. *It's Kind of a Cute Story.* Bamboo Forest Publishing, 2012.

Disney Institute. *Be Our Guest: Perfecting the Art of Customer Service.* New York, NY: Disney Editions, 2001.

Dixon, Jeff. *The Disney-Driven Life: Inspiring Lessons from Disney History.* Orlando, FL: Theme Park Press, 2016.

Dunlop, Beth. *Building A Dream: The Art of Disney Architecture.* New York, NY: Harry N. Abrams, 1996.

Eisner, Michael. *Work in Progress: Risking Failure, Surviving Success.* New York, NY: Hyperion, 2011.

Emerson, Chad Denver. *Project Future: The Inside Story Behind the Creation of Disney World.* Charleston, SC: Ayefour, 2010.

Emerson, Ralph Waldo. "Self-Reliance." *Self-Reliance and Other Essays.* New York, NY: Dover Books, 2012.

Ferriss, Timothy. *Tools of Titans: The Tactics, Routines, and Habits of Billionaires, Icons, and World-Class Performers.* Boston, MA: Houghton Mifflin Harcourt, 2016.

Finch, Christopher. *Walt Disney's America.* New York, NY: Abbeville Press, 1978.

Foglesong, Richard E. *Married to the Mouse: Walt Disney World and Orlando.* New Haven, CT: Yale University Press, 2001.

France, Van Arsdale. *Window on Main Street: 35 Years of Creating Happiness at Disneyland Park.* Orlando, FL: Theme Park Press, 2015.

Francaviglia, Richard V. *Main Street Revisited: Time, Space, and Image Building in Small-Town America.* Iowa City: U of Iowa P, 1996.

Gabler, Neal. *Walt Disney: The Triumph of the American Imagination.* New York, NY: Random House, 2006.

Gennawey, Sam. *The Disneyland Story: The Unofficial Guide to the Evolution of Walt Disney's Dream.* Birmingham, AL: Keen Communications, 2014.

Gennawey, Sam. *JayBangs: How Jay Stein, MCA, & Universal Invented the Modern Theme Park and Beat Disney at Its Own Game.* Orlando, FL: Theme Park Press, 2016.

Gennawey, Sam. *Walt Disney and the Promise of Progress City.* Orlando, FL: Theme Park Press, 2014.

Ghez, Didier. *Walt's People: Volume 11: Talking Disney with the Artists Who Knew Him.* Orlando, FL: Theme Park Press, 2013.

Ghez, Didier. *Walt's People: Volume 17: Talking Disney with the Artists Who Knew Him.* Orlando, FL: Theme Park Press, 2015.

Gitomer, Jeffrey. *Customer Satisfaction Is Worthless, Customer Loyalty Is Priceless: How to Make Customers Love You, Keep Them Coming Back and Tell Everyone They Know.* Austin, TX: Bard Press, 1998.

Goins, Jeff. *The Art of Work.* Nashville, TN: Nelson Books, 2015.

Grazer, Brian, and Charles Fishman. *A Curious Mind: The Secret to a Bigger*

Life. New York: Simon & Schuster Paperbacks, 2016.

Guise, Stephen. *Mini Habits: Small Habits, Bigger Results*. n.p.: CreateSpace, 2013.

Haas, Charlie. "Disneyland Is Good for You." *New West*. December 4, 1978. p. 13-19.

Haidt, Jonathan. *The Happiness Hypothesis*. New York, NY: Basic Books, 2006.

Harvey, Steve. *Act Like a Success, Think Like a Success: Discovering Your Gift and the Way to Life's Riches*. New York, NY: Amistad, 2014.

Hayzlett, Jeffrey W. *Think Big, Act Bigger: The Rewards of Being Relentless*. Irvine, CA: Entrepreneur, 2015.

Hench, John. *Designing Disney: Imagineering and the Art of the Show*. New York, NY: Disney Editions, 2003.

Hendricks, Gay. *The Big Leap: Conquer Your Hidden Fear and Take Life to the Next Level*. New York: HarperCollins, 2010.

Holiday, Ryan. *Ego Is the Enemy*. New York: Portfolio/Penguin, 2016.

Holiday, Ryan. *The Obstacle Is the Way: The Timeless Art of Turning Trials into Triumph*. New York: Portfolio/Penguin, 2014.

Imagineers, The. *Walt Disney Imagineering: A Behind the Dreams Look at Making MORE Magic Real*. New York, NY: Disney Editions, 2009.

Imagineers, The. *Walt Disney Imagineering: A Behind the Dreams Look at Making the Magic Real*. New York, NY: Hyperion, 1996.

Jackson, Kathy Merlock and Mark West, eds. *Disneyland and Culture: Essays on the Parks and Their Influence*. Jefferson, NC: McFarland & Company, 2011.

Jackson, Kathy Merlock and Mark I. West, eds. *Walt Disney, from Reader to Storyteller: Essays on the Literary Inspirations*. Jefferson, NC: McFarland & Co., 2015.

Keller, Gary. *The One Thing: The Surprisingly Simple Truth behind Extraordinary Results*. London: John Murray, 2014.

Kingston, Karen. *Clear Your Clutter with Feng Shui (Revised and Updated): Free Yourself from Physical, Mental, Emotional, and Spiritual Clutter Forever*. New York, NY: Random House, LLC, 2016.

Knight, Sarah. *Get Your Sh*t Together: How to Stop Worrying About What You Should Do So You Can Finish What You Need to Do and Start Doing What You Want to Do (A No F*cks Given Guide)*. Boston, MA: Little, Brown and Company, 2016.

Knight, Sarah. *The Life-Changing Magic of Not Giving a F*ck: How to Stop Spending Time You Don't Have with People You Don't Like Doing Things You Don't Want to Do (A No F*cks Given Guide)*. Boston, MA: Little, Brown and Company, 2015.

Koenig, David. *Mouse Tales: A Behind-The-Ears Look at Disneyland*. Irvine, CA: Bonaventure Press, 1994.

Koenig, David. *More Mouse Tales: A Closer Peek Backstage at Disneyland*. Irvine, CA: Bonaventure Press, 1999.

Koenig, David. *Realityland: True-Life Adventures at Walt Disney World*. Irvine, CA: Bonadventure Press, 2007.

Kondo, Marie. *The Life-Changing Magic of Tidying Up: The Japanese Art of Decluttering and Organizing*. New York, NY: Random House, 2014.

Korkis, Jim. *How to Be a Disney Historian: Tips from the Top Professionals*. Orlando, FL: Theme Park Press, 2016.

Korkis, Jim. *The Revised Vault of Walt: Unofficial, Unauthorized, Uncensored Disney Stories Never Told*. Orlando, FL: Theme Park Press, 2012.

Korkis, Jim. *More Secret Stories of Walt Disney World: More Things You Never Knew You Never Knew*. Orlando, FL: Theme Park, 2016.

Korkis, Jim. *Secret Stories of Disneyland: Trivia Notes, Quotes, and Anecdotes*. Orlando, FL: Theme Park Press, 2017.

Korkis, Jim. *Secret Stories of Walt Disney World: Things You Never Knew You Never Knew*. Orlando, FL: Theme Park, 2015.

Korkis, Jim. *The Unofficial Disneyland 1955 Companion: The Anecdotal Story of the Birth of the Happiest Place on Earth*. Orlando, FL: Theme Park Press, 2016.

Korkis, Jim. *The Vault of Walt*. Orlando, FL: Theme Park Press, 2010.

Korkis, Jim. *The Vault of Walt: Volume 2*. Orlando, FL: Theme Park Press, 2013.

Korkis, Jim. *The Vault of Walt: Volume 3*. Orlando, FL: Theme Park Press, 2014.

Korkis, Jim. *The Value of Walt: Volume 4*. Orlando, FL: Theme Park Press, 2015.

Korkis, Jim. *The Value of Walt: Volume 5*. Orlando, FL: Theme Park Press, 2016.

Korkis, Jim. *Walt's Words: Quotations of Walt Disney with Sources*. Orlando, FL: Theme Park Press, 2016.

Kurtti, Jeff. *Since the World Began: Walt Disney World, the First 25 Years*. New York: Hyperion, 1996.

Lefkin, Wendy, ed. *Disney Insider Yearbook: 2005 Year in Review*. New York, NY: Disney Editions, Inc., 2006.

Lindquist, Jack, and Melinda J. Combs. *In Service to the Mouse: My Unexpected Journey to Becoming Disneyland's First President: A Memoir*. Orange, CA: Neverland Media and Chapman UP, 2010.

Lipp, Doug. *Disney U: How Disney University Develops the World's Most Engaged, Loyal, and Customer-Centric Employees*. New York, NY: McGraw-Hill, 2013.

Mackenzie, Mindy. *The Courage Solution: The Power of Truth Telling with Your Boss, Peers, and Team*. Greenleaf Book Group Press, 2016.

Marling, Karal Ann. *Designing Disney's Theme Parks: The Architecture of*

Reassurance. New York, NY: Flammarion, 1997.

McRaven. William H. *Make Your Bed.* New York, NY: Grand Central Publishing, 2017.

Miller, Donald. *A Million Miles in a Thousand Years: What I Learned While Editing My Life.* Nashville, TN: Thomas Nelson Publishers, 2009.

Mumford, David and Bruce Gordon. *Disneyland the Nickel Tour: A Postcard Journey Through 40 Years of the Happiest Place on Earth.* Camphor Tree Publisher, 1995.

Nabbe, Tom. *From Disneyland's Tom Sawyer to Disney Legend: The Adventures of Tom Nabbe.* Orlando, FL: Theme Park Press, 2015.

Niles, Robert. *Stories from a Theme Park Insider.* Niles Online, 2011.

O'Brien, Tim. *Tony Baxter: First of the Second Generation of Walt Disney Imagineers.* Nashville, TN: Casa Flamingo Literary Arts, 2015.

Pausch, Randy and Jeffrey Zaslow. *The Last Lecture.* Hachette Books, 2008.

Pierce, Todd James. *Three Years in Wonderland: The Disney Brothers, C.V. Wood and the Making of the Great American Theme Park.* UP of Mississippi, 2016.

Pressfield, Steven. *Do the Work!: Overcome Resistance and Get Out of Your Own Way.* The Domino Project, 2011.

Pressfield, Steven. *Turning Pro: Tap Your Inner Power and Create Your Life's Work.* New York, NY: Black Irish Entertainment, 2012.

Pressfield, Steven. *The War of Art: Break Through the Blocks and Win Your Inner Creative Battles.* New York, NY: Black Irish Entertainment, 2002.

Prosperi, Lou. *The Imagineering Pyramid: Using Disney Theme Park Design Principles to Develop and Promote Your Creative Ideas.* Orlando, FL: Theme Park Press, 2016.

Robbins, Mel. *The 5 Second Rule: Transform Your Life, Work, and Confidence with Everyday Courage.* Savio Republic, 2017.

Rubens, Tom. *Lifeness: Harmonizing an Entrepreneurial Life.* BSB Publishing, 2017.

Schultz, Jason and Kevin Yee. *Disneyland Almanac: Complete Park Information 1955-2010.* Zauberreich Press, 2011.

Sehlinger, Bob, Seth Kubersky, and Len Testa. *The Unofficial Guide to Disneyland 2013.* Birmingham, AL: Keen Communications, LLC, 2013.

Sincero, Jen. *You Are a Badass at Making Money: Master the Mindset of Wealth.* New York, NY: John Murray Learning, 2017.

Sincero, Jen. *You Are a Badass: How to Stop Doubting Your Greatness and Start Living Your Awesome Life.* Philadelphia, PA: Running Press, 2013.

Sinek, Simon. *Leaders Eat Last: Why Some Teams Pull Together and Others Don't.* New York, NY: Penguin, 2014.

Sinek, Simon. *Start with Why: How Great Leaders Inspire Everyone to Take Action.* New York, NY: Portfolio/Penguin, 2009.

Sisneros, Dan. *Disney Tale of the Tape: Theme Park Boxing.* Amazon Digital Services, 2016.

Sivers, Derek. *Anything You Want: 40 Lessons for a New Kind of Entrepreneur.* New York, NY: Penguin, 2015.

Sklar, Marty. *Dream It! Do It!: My Half-Century Creating Disney's Magic Kingdoms.* New York, NY: Disney Editions, 2013.

Sklar, Marty, and Richard M. Sherman. *One Little Spark!: Mickey's Ten Commandments and the Road to Imagineering.* Los Angeles: Disney Editions, 2015.

Smith, Dave, ed. *The Quotable Walt Disney.* New York, NY: Disney Editions, 2001.

Smith, Christopher E. *The Walt Disney World that Never Was: Stories Behind the Amazing Imagineering Dreams that Never Came True.* Orlando, FL: Theme Park Press, 2016.

Smith, Dave. *Disney A to Z: The Official Encyclopedia*. 5th ed. Los Angeles, CA: Disney Editions, 2016.

Strodder, Chris. *The Disneyland Book of Lists: Unofficial, Unauthorized, and Unprecedented*. Solano Beach, CA: Santa Monica Press, 2015.

Strodder, Chris. *The Disneyland Encyclopedia: The Unofficial, Unauthorized, and Unprecedented History of Every Land, Attraction, Restaurant, Shop, and Major Event in the Original Magic Kingdom*. Solano Beach, CA: Santa Monica Press, 2012.

Sullivan, William "Sully," and Jim Korkis. *From Jungle Cruise Skipper to Disney Legend: 40 Years of Magical Memories at Disney*. Orlando, FL: Theme Park, 2015.

Susanin, Timothy S. *Walt Before Mickey: Disney's Early Years, 1919-1928*. UP of Mississippi, 2011.

Tevelow, Jesse. *Hustle: The Life-Changing Effects of Constant Motion*. Amazon Digital Services LLC, 2015.

Thomas, Bob. *Walt Disney: An American Original*. New York, NY: Disney Editions, 1994.

"Walt Disney From Mickey to the Magic Kingdom." *Life Magazine*. 15 Jul 2016.

Williams, Pat and Jim Denney. *How to Be Like Walt: Capturing the Disney Magic Every Day of Your Life*. Health Communications, 2004.

Wiseman, Richard. *59 Seconds: Think a Little, Change a Lot*. New York: Alfred A. Knopf, 2009.

Wright, Alex. *The Imagineering Field Guide to Disney California Adventure at Disneyland: An Imagineer's-Eye Tour*. Glendale, CA: Disney Editions, 2014.

Wright, Alex. *The Imagineering Field Guide to Disneyland*. New York, NY: Disney Editions, 2008.

Wright, Alex. *The Imagineering Field Guide to Epcot at Walt Disney World: An*

Imagineer's-Eye Tour. New York, NY: Disney Editions, 2010.

Wright, Alex. *The Imagineering Field Guide to Disney's Hollywood Studios at Walt Disney World: An Imagineer's-Eye Tour.* New York, NY: Disney Editions, 2010.

Wright, Alex. *The Imagineering Field Guide to the Magic Kingdom at Walt Disney World: An Imagineer's-Eye Tour.* New York, NY: Disney, 2010.

Wright, Alex. *The Imagineering Field Guide to Disney's Animal Kingdom at Walt Disney World: An Imagineer's-Eye Tour.* New York, NY: Disney Enterprises, 2007.

FILM, TELEVISION, AND MUSEUM RESOURCES

Disneyland. TV Show. ABC. 1954-1958.

Disneyland Secrets, Stories and Magic. DVD. Walt Disney Video, 2007.

The Disney Family Museum, San Francisco, California.

Tony Robbins: I Am Not Your Guru. Netflix, 2016.

Walt Disney Treasures: Disneyland USA. DVD. Walt Disney Video, 2001.

WEBSITES

https://bgavideo.wordpress.com/2008/10/23/disney-design-forced-perspective/

http://deepexistence.com/

https://disneyinstitute.com/blog/2013/10/letting-go-leadership-lessons-from-walt-disney/211/

http://freshbakeddisney.com

http://www.hiddenmickeys.org

http://www.jimhillmedia.com

http://www.jonathanfields.com

http://www.justdisney.com/walt_disney/biography/long_bio.html

http://www.laparks.org/dos/parks/griffithpk/mgr.htm

http://www.latimes.com/travel/themeparks/la-trb-disneyland-2055-20141223-story.html#page=1

http://www.laughingplace.com

http://www.leavingconformitycoaching.com

http://www.micechat.com

http://www.mouseplanet.com

http://www.ocregister.com/

http://samlanddisney.blogspot.com

http://www.tabletmag.com/jewish-arts-and-culture/206125/elie-wiesel-visits-disneyland

http://www.ted.com/speakers/tim_brown

http://www.themedattraction.com

http://www.themeparkinsider.com

http://tomnabbe.com

http://tonyrobbins.com

http://wdwfacts.com

http://www.wdwinfo.com

http://www.yesterland.com

CPSIA information can be obtained
at www.ICGtesting.com
Printed in the USA
BVHW041146210319
543341BV00014B/79/P